Boundaries
and
Relationships

Other Books by Charles L. Whitfield

Healing The Child Within

A Gift To Myself

Co-dependence

My Recovery Plan — Stage 1, 2 and 3
(booklets)

BOUNDARIES AND RELATIONSHIPS

Knowing, Protecting and Enjoying the Self

Charles L. Whitfield, M.D.

Health Communications, Inc.
Deerfield Beach, Florida

Charles L. Whitfield, M.D.
Box 420487
Atlanta, GA 30342
404-843-4300

Library of Congress Cataloging-in-Publication Data

Whitfield, Charles L.
    Boundaries and relationships: knowing, protecting, and enjoying
the self/by Charles L. Whitfield.
      p.   cm.
    Includes bibliographical references and index.
    ISBN 1-55874-259-X
    1. Interpersonal relations. 2. Self. I. Title.
HM132.W5   1993   92-40512
158'.2—dc20   CIP

© 1993 Charles L. Whitfield
ISBN 1-55874-259-X

Publisher: Health Communications, Inc.
            3201 S.W. 15th Street
            Deerfield Beach, FL 33442-8190

Cover design by Barbara M. Bergman

Acknowledgments

Grateful thanks and acknowledgment for permission to use or quote material from the following sources:

Karen Paine-Gernee and Terry Hunt for two quotes from their book *Emotional Healing*, Warner Books, NY, copyright by the authors, 1990.

Barbara Harris for an edited reproduction of the chapter on boundaries from her book *Spiritual Awakenings: A Guidebook for Experiencers* published by Stage 3, 1993, copyright by the author, 1993.

Rokelle Lerner for a quote from her booklet "Boundaries for Codependents" from Hazelden, Center City, MN, copyright by the author, 1988.

Marilyn Mason for her concepts on intimacy from her booklet on "Intimacy" from Hazelden, Center City, MN, copyright by the author, 1986.

Greg Lawson for his cartoon on fusion, copyright by the artist, 1989.

Art Bouthillier for his cartoon on making a wall, copyright by the artist, date unknown.

Romaine Brooks for her drawing on the parents enmeshing the children, Smithsonian Institution Press, copyright by the artist, 1986.

Salvador Minuchin for his observations on boundaries and the quote from his book *Families and Family Therapy*, Harvard University Press, copyright by the author, 1974.

Michael Kerr and Murray Bowen for their concepts on triangles and two illustrations from their book *Family Evaluations* W.W. Norton, NY, copyright by the authors, 1988.

Tom Fogarty for his concepts and quotations from his articles on Fusion and Triangles from *Compendium I*, Center for Family Learning, New Rochelle, NY, copyright by the author 1973-78.

Ken Wilber for his concepts and a quote from his book *No Boundary*, copyright by the author, 1978.

Robert Frost for permission to reprint his poem "Mending Wall," copyright by Holt Rinehart & Winston, NY, 1963.

Marsha Utain for her description of roles and boundaries in getting out of triangles from her booklet "Stepping Out Of Chaos," Health Communications, copyright by the author 1989.

Culver Pictures Inc. for woodcut of The Magician.

Special thanks to John Amodeo, Jean Kiljian, Herb Gravitz, Sally Merchant, Vicki Mermelstein and Barbara Harris for their review and suggestions for improvement on this book. Also to Mary Johnston for her excellent typing and Marie Stilkind for her superb editing.

Cover Art by Andre Jacques Victor Orsel (1795-1850). Courtesy of Brandt Dayton & Co. Ltd., New York. The position of the man's head is lower than the woman's, and even though this may subconsciously suggest an unequal relationship, the publisher and I decided to reproduce the painting in its original form — CLW

Contents

Figures and Tables

Tables

What This Book is About

I wrote this book for both the general reader and the helping professional to describe just why and how personal boundaries are useful in numerous aspects of recovery and life, including obtaining peace and serenity. Boundaries are crucial in recovery from the toxic effects of nearly all unhealthy relationships, diseases and conditions. The following is a brief description of what is in this book.

Introduction, Overview and Personal Boundary Survey

In the first chapter I give an Introduction and Overview of boundaries and limits in a person's life. What are boundaries? What areas of our life can they affect? And how can we make use of them in our relationships? In Chapter 2 the reader has an opportunity to check out the status of their own personal boundaries by answering several questions that apply to their everyday life. I supplement this survey with a description of the dynamics of each question.

History and Origins from a Developmental Perspective

Chapter 3 provides a brief history of how theorists, teachers and helping professionals have viewed boundaries over the past 2500 years. Then Chapter 4 describes how boundaries become healthy or unhealthy — the origins of boundaries — from a

developmental perspective. How do we develop unhealthy boundaries? Healthy boundaries? And what can we do to heal our
boundary problems?

Age Regression

To me, Chapter 5 is one of the most basic and helpful, wherein
I describe the powerful phenomenon of Age Regression and show
how boundaries are crucial in healing its psychological damage.
It is here that we can begin to gain great insight and understanding about ourselves and begin to transform our unhealthy
relationships.

Giving and Receiving in Relationships: Projective Identification

The next three chapters, numbers 6, 7 and 8, contain a concise
description of what I call "giving and receiving," a part of which
therapists call Projective Identification — and a key to avoiding
unhealthy relationships. Here we look into some practical steps
that I can take to sort out whenever there is a conflict in a
relationship, just what material in that conflict is mine and what
is not mine. This is crucial information to help me have healthy
relationships.

Characteristics of Healthy Boundaries

In Chapter 9 I describe the Characteristics or Markers of
healthy boundaries and limits. How can I recognize them? How
can I know a healthy boundary from an unhealthy one?

Basic Dynamics and Core Issues in Relationships

In Chapter 10 I review some Basic Dynamics, such as pursuing
and distancing in relationships, and show how boundaries interact
with each of these basic dynamics. In Chapters 11 and 12 I describe our core life and recovery issues and show how they also
involve boundaries and limits.

Triangles

Triangles can aggravate the harmony in a relationship. Chapters 13 and 14 show a simplified approach to recognizing and

understanding triangles, wherein I may find myself involved in a painful or conflicted three-way relationship, and how to get out of and even avoid them.

The Process of Recovery and Spirituality

But how does all of this material relate to the Process of Recovery and healing? This is what I describe in Chapter 15. In Chapter 16, entitled " 'No' is a Complete Sentence," I show additional ways of setting healthy boundaries and limits, including being assertive. And in Chapter 17 I discuss some practical perspectives on Spirituality and Boundaries.

Because boundaries are related to the psycho-spiritual energy of the body, I have included in the Appendix an exciting and useful approach to this topic by author and researcher Barbara Harris.

I believe that this book offers a new and expanded perspective on the importance of boundaries and limits in relationships. This is because most of what is in this book is not included or discussed in this detail or approach in any other book. Whether you are seeking to improve your relationships or you are a helping professional who assists people in any aspect of the process of healing, I hope that you will find this book to be useful.

Charles L. Whitfield, M.D.
Baltimore
April 1993

———— • ————
Foreword
by John Amodeo, Ph.D.

When I first read Charles Whitfield's classic book, *Healing the Child Within*, I was impressed by the clarity and skill of his writing. He has shone a new light on the vital theme of re-awakening to our authentic True Self. In this book he directs our attention to the equally vital task of creating boundaries to protect and nurture that Real Self.

A boundary marks the place where my reality ends and where yours begins. That may seem obvious. But the key question is this: What does it *mean* that you and I are two distinct unique individuals? What are the implications for how we relate to ourselves and others?

Our inner life consists of our feelings, thoughts, needs and wants, as well as our values, our hopes and our dreams — what is important and meaningful to us. These are vital aspects of who we are. They comprise some major aspects of what Whitfield calls our True Self. No one can take that from us.

Contacting and living from our True Self is the central task of personal growth. But being real and genuine is easier said than done, for it places us in a vulnerable position in relation to others. It exposes us to the dreaded possibility of being criticized, rejected and hurt. These affronts to our sensitive soul may send us scurrying back into a cell of bitter pain and isolation, where we feel worthless, inadequate and inferior. We then feel unsafe to show our Authentic Self.

Those of us who've been rejected, abandoned or betrayed know the pain that results from being open with others, only to be treated harshly and coldly. As a result, we may retreat deep within ourselves. We may go into hiding and conceal our innermost feelings, hopes and longings from others, and oftentimes, even from ourselves. Sadly, we decide not to trust. We feel unsafe to love and be loved.

Rather than close down to the hurts of our heart, we can choose a more hopeful path — one that is the subject of this book: the path of setting personal boundaries. Learning to set clear boundaries with others enables us to affirm and be ourselves in a world that is often insensitive to us, whether intentionally or not. Boundaries provide the protection we need in order to negotiate the difficult and painful junctures we encounter in daily life.

Growing confident in our ability to establish healthy boundaries enables us to affirm and honor ourselves. Then, if we are unfairly attacked, blamed, rejected or mistreated, we're not required to be passive victims, as perhaps we were in the past. As we draw upon inner resources, we can respond from our strength, rather than slinking into a tired sense of worthlessness, despair or cynicism.

Submitting to others, rather than affirming our own reality, is the heart of active co-dependence — we give up our own inner world in order to be accepted by others. Such co-dependence amounts to a self-betrayal. We give up ourselves in order to please, satisfy or impress others. By betraying our True Self, our sense of integrity and wholeness suffers. Our spirit wilts. Having healthy boundaries enables us to move from self-betrayal to self-affirmation, self-regard and self-trust.

By protecting our genuine, authentic self, boundaries help us feel freer and safer to be our Genuine Self — to express our real feelings, wants and viewpoints. We can affirm our inner world while granting others the right to have *their* feelings, thoughts, needs and viewpoints, which might be different from our own. Through healthy boundaries, we ask to be treated with respect, while extending respect to others.

Boundaries protect us. But they don't keep us distant and separate from people. Just the opposite. They provide a foundation for sound, healthy intimacy. A relationship requires two people who are relating to each other. Lacking awareness of our inner world, we remain enmeshed, not intimate. We fuse with the other's universe of feelings, wants and desires. Losing sight of our own inner life, we may later feel resentful because we have not been true to ourselves. We have not taken time to notice what we really want. This dis-serves not only ourselves, but others as well. When we have delayed setting boundaries, we may establish them later with a vengeance. This may escalate conflict or lead to betrayal or abandonment.

By learning to calibrate our boundaries, we decide who to let close to us, as well as how close we want them to be. Through our experience, we come to know our "yes" and our "no," which may be quite different from others' "yes" and "no." When we feel safe and comfortable, we can allow ourselves to be intimate. Or we can talk about how we feel unsafe or distant, which might resolve conflicts or differences that disrupt closeness.

The most effective boundaries are flexible ones. We can be assertive without being aggressive. We can express what we want and how we feel in a straightforward way, while also being sensitive to the effects of our words upon others. We can be tender and strong, firm and respectful. We can learn to dialogue with others in a spirit of mutual openness and discovery. Boundaries are not a weapon to be used against others. They are a way of being ourselves while also being in relationship.

This important book explores the basic and often subtle facets of boundaries. As we develop an awareness of boundaries, we discover how others may be mistreating us, or how we may be mistreating others. (Is it their stuff or my stuff?) We set limits regarding the unacceptable behavior of others. We discover the core issues that lead us to ignore and overlook our actual experience. We avoid unhealthy triangles — destructive alliances against third parties. We discover how past wounds may prevent us from standing up to present mistreatment. These and other important facets of boundaries are addressed in this book with clarity and caring — by a highly regarded therapist and teacher in the areas of co-dependence and recovery.

We have a right to know and set boundaries with others. In fact, we have a responsibility to do so — both to ourselves and others. Boundaries are necessary for love and intimacy. They allow us to love ourselves, while simultaneously protecting and nurturing our cherished relationships. This book covers new ground in assisting us to find a middle path between submission and dominance in our relationships. Committed to balancing love and caring for our self with love and caring for others, we will develop new understandings that will enable us to walk the razor's edge between being our real selves and being in healthy relationships.

1
Introduction
And Overview

Being aware of our boundaries and limits is useful in our relationships and recovery. In fact, this awareness is *crucial* to having healthy relationships and a successful recovery.

A boundary or limit is *how far we can go with comfort* in a relationship. It delineates where I and my physical and psychological space end and where you and yours begin. Boundary is a concept that provokes a real experience within us. Therefore, in my relationships with people, places and things, the boundary is real. My boundaries and limits are real. The other's boundaries and limits are real.

In describing boundaries, Paine and Hunt say, "Interaction with others occurs at boundaries — yours and theirs — where you end and they begin. The easiest way to understand healthy functioning of boundaries is to think of the role of cells. The cell wall is a semipermeable membrane. When it functions correctly, the cell wall keeps poisons out, lets nutrients in, and excretes waste. It also defines the existence of the cell by separating it from other cells. Healthy cells have an intelligence that knows whether to be a stomach cell or a brain cell.

1

"Healthy cells demonstrate good contact at their boundaries by discriminating between nutrition and poison, and by positioning and duplicating themselves. The healthy person must do the same. To have a semipermeable membrane, to know when to allow in and when to keep out, means you have a choice in your life, and means you will be an active rather than a passive participant in it. To manage contact well is an expression of self, integrity, and freedom."[86]

A similar example is the body's immune system, which functions to maintain the boundary of the body's unique individuality, distinguishing and keeping out what is "not me" and holding in place what is "me."[77]

Having an awareness of boundaries and limits helps me discover *who I am*. Until I know who I am, it will be difficult for me to have healthy relationships, whether they may be casual acquaintances, friends, close relationships or intimate relationships. Figure 1.1 shows a simple diagram of a healthy boundary.

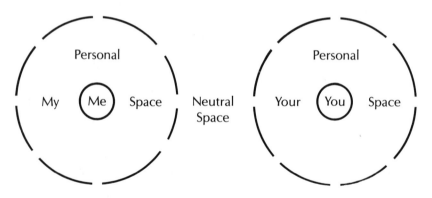

Figure 1.1. A Healthy Boundary

Without an awareness of healthy boundaries, it will be difficult for me to sort out who is unsafe to be around, which may include people who are toxic for me, and even some people who may mistreat or abuse me. Figure 1.2 shows a diagram of an absent, unhealthy, or blurred boundary.

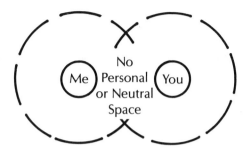

Figure 1.2. An Unhealthy Boundary

The boundary marks or delineates the differences between me and the other. Without boundaries, it would be hard to define my self. Without them, it would be hard to know myself. Without boundaries, I may not feel that I have a self. And without boundaries, I can't have a healthy self. So by being aware of and having healthy boundaries, I can define and know myself, know that I have a self, and have a healthy self.

My Inner Life

A key to my boundaries is *knowing my inner life.* My inner life includes my beliefs, thoughts, feelings, decisions, choices and experiences. It also includes my wants, needs, sensations within my body, my intuitions and even unconscious factors in my life. If I am unaware of or out of touch with my inner life, I can't know all of my boundaries and limits. When I am aware of my inner life, I can more readily know my boundaries (Figure 1.3).

The actively co-dependent person tends to be fixed in either few or no boundaries, *boundarylessness,* or the opposite, *overly rigid boundaries.* And they often flip-flop between these. Because they focus so much of their attention outside of themselves, they tend to be less aware of their inner life, and thus less aware of their boundaries.[112]

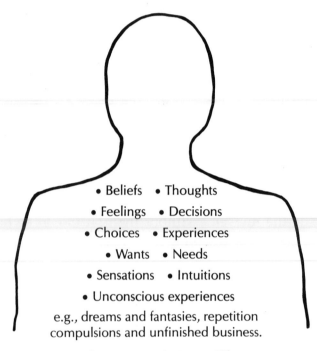

- Beliefs • Thoughts
- Feelings • Decisions
- Choices • Experiences
- Wants • Needs
- Sensations • Intuitions
- Unconscious experiences
e.g., dreams and fantasies, repetition
compulsions and unfinished business.

Figure 1.3. My Inner Life

Flexibility and Adaptability

Another key to having healthy boundaries is flexibility and adaptability. When we are able to be flexible and adaptable in any relationship — without being mistreated or abused — we can know ourselves in a deeper and richer way. And we can let go more easily into the experience of that relationship to enjoy both its fun aspects and its growth points.

In our day-to-day experience we have many opportunities for growth. That growth includes the physical, mental, emotional and spiritual realms of our awareness, experience and consciousness. Awareness of our boundaries helps us in that growth.

Not being sufficiently aware of their inner life, the unrecovered and actively co-dependent person may be so flexible and adaptable that they are flexible and adaptable even when they are being mistreated or abused. Unaware of their True Self — their Child Within — and its crucial inner life, they let people mistreat or abuse them. They are unable or unwilling to set boundaries or limits and stick with them. And so they suffer unnecessarily. Setting healthy boundaries and limits is a way to deal with and prevent unnecessary pain and suffering.*

Specific Boundaries

We can have a relationship, whether transient or long-term, with nearly any person, place or thing. To make those relationships go better, we can use boundaries and limits in a healthy way in many areas of our lives. These areas include the physical, mental, emotional and spiritual realms of our life. I list these areas and some specific examples of factors in each where boundaries can be helpful in Table 1.1. I may invade another's boundaries by interpreting, manipulating or invading any of these boundary factors. Another person may invade my boundaries by doing the same to me.

Physical Areas of Our Life

Included in the physical area is a broad range of simple and complex boundary factors. Some simple ones are pollution (such as noise or smoke), clothes, food and shelter. More complex are those such as money, property, gifts and physical differentness from others. Regarding any of these, can you recall any times when your boundaries were invaded? (Feel free to write about any of these, or those above

---

* The *True* or *Real Self,* which I also call the *Child Within,* is our true identity, who we really are. It has also been called the existential self, the heart or soul. It is to be differentiated from the *false self,* ego or co-dependent self, which I develop in *Healing the Child Within, A Gift to Myself* and *Co-dependence — Healing the Human Condition.*

or below, in any of the blank spaces in this book or in your journal or diary.) Even more complex are such things as physical closeness, touching, sexual behavior, eye contact, privacy, time and energy.

Table 1.1. Some Factors in Boundaries in Relationships

Type of Boundary

Physical	Mental/Emotional	Spiritual
Physical closeness	Beliefs	Personal experiences
Touching	Thoughts and ideas	Relationship with
Sexual behavior	Feelings	True Self, Higher
Eye contact	Decisions	Self and Higher
Privacy — mail,	Choices	Power
diary, doors, nudity,	Unfinished business	Spirituality
bathroom, telephone,	Projections	Religion
private spaces, etc.	Energy	Spiritual path
Clothes	Sexuality	Spiritual preferences
Shelter	Needs	Spiritual practices
Property	Time alone	
Money	Intuitions	
Physical	Individual differences	
differences	Love	
Gifts	Interests	
Food	Relationships	
Pollution —	Responsibilities	
e.g., noise	Confidences	
and smoke	Secrets	
Time and energy	Participation	
	Roles	
	Rules	
	Messenger function	

Some of these areas can be inter-related and thereby become more complex. An example follows:

> **Cathy** (whose history is also described on pages 34 to 36 of *Healing the Child Within*) was a 32-year-old woman who grew up in a troubled family. As a little girl she frequently

had her *privacy* boundaries invaded. For example, when she was in the bathroom brushing her teeth or combing her hair, her father would often come in and urinate next to her, without even noticing that she was uncomfortable or that doing so was not appropriate. It was a boundary invasion.

When she grew up, she had much difficulty with relationships with men. She also showed and experienced high tolerance for inappropriate behavior. These difficulties ranged from her accepting men making inappropriate verbal remarks and physical passes at her, to fear and discomfort when having sex with her fiance.

Cathy suffered unnecessarily with these until one day in group therapy. As she was describing the above aspects of her childhood, she got feedback from the group that her father's behavior was inappropriate, that this was indeed *covert sexual abuse.* On hearing this, she became so choked up that she started wheezing in her throat, something she had not done before in group. The choking and wheezing became so intense that she had to stand up and walk around the room. (This reaction is an example of an *abreaction,* which is a sudden experiencing and discharging of painful feelings and often painful somatic sensations associated with the bringing to awareness of an ungrieved hurt or trauma).*

The group accepted and supported her through this abreaction. This event and the group's support permitted her to work further, both in and outside of the group, on her boundary invasions by men. Since doing so, she has been able to set limits with men who invade her boundaries in these ways, and she is no longer intimidated by them. This work has also given her an opening to work more on boundaries and limits with women in her life.

---

* Have you ever experienced an abreaction of any kind? If you remember any, feel free to write about them in any of the blank spaces in this book or in your journal or diary. Also, consider telling someone safe about them. (See page 102 of this book and page 35 in *A Gift to Myself* if you are not clear on the description of safe people.) I discuss abreaction in more detail on page 86.

Mental and Emotional Areas of our Life

Mental and emotional boundaries include many important aspects of our lives (Table 1.1). Some of these are our beliefs, thoughts, ideas, feelings, decisions and choices. For example, have you ever been told what you "should" believe, think, feel, decide or choose? If so, then your boundaries may have been invaded at that time.

Has anyone ever accused you of or blamed you for something that they did or that was actually their issue? How did you feel when they did that? They may have been invading your boundaries by *projecting* some of their unfinished business or issues onto you. Did you buy into it? Are you still tolerating it? You don't have to. Their pain, confusion or attempts at control or manipulation may be theirs, not yours. With awareness of your inner life and with clear boundaries and limits, you can handle or at times even prevent such a boundary invasion, and thus avoid unnecessary pain and suffering. A key to understanding all of the above is the dynamic of age regression, which I describe in Chapter 5.

Other mental and emotional areas where personal boundaries are important include our energy, sexuality, needs, time alone, intuitions and even our individual differences. Has anyone ever drained your energy so much that you neglected your own needs? Possibility: You may have experienced a lack of awareness of your inner life, including your needs. You may have been people-pleasing to the detriment of self (active co-dependence). This is a set-up for boundary violation and more unnecessary pain and suffering.

Has anyone criticized you because you do things differently from them? Or criticized you for some aspect of your sexuality? If so, how did you feel? And what happened? What did you do with the resulting conflict? Did you work it through directly with the other person? And if appropriate, did you set limits with them? Or did you hold in your feelings, possibly to avoid their confronting or rejecting you?

Some other mental and emotional areas where personal boundaries are helpful include: love, interests, relationships, participation, roles, rules and messenger function. *Messenger function* means that someone inappropriately convinces you to deliver a message to a third party. And if you do so, you might end up with more than you bargained for, e.g., more unnecessary pain and suffering. Of course, such suffering may turn out to be useful if you work through the conflict or issue and learn from it, including setting limits with the other person so that it doesn't happen again.

But these and other areas in relationships are often not so simple and clear-cut. For example, have you ever declined interest in something that is being pushed on you by another (which is a potential boundary invasion)? Then you later became interested in and perhaps even profited by whatever they had been promoting? A principle we can use is to keep our boundaries as flexible as feels appropriate for us — for our wants and needs and other aspects of our inner life — and take responsibility for our risking and for consciously setting a healthy boundary or withdrawing if we wish. This is another example of using our boundaries in a healthy way.

Spiritual

Some spiritual areas where boundaries may apply include our own spirituality and personal experiences, whether of an obviously spiritual nature or not. A major area regards our relationship with our True Self, our Divine or Higher Self, and our Higher Power. Some fundamentalist religious people may tell others they can't have a relationship with their Higher Self, because it is "demonic" or not consistent with their interpretation of the scriptures. Is their doing so a boundary invasion? If you sense in your heart that you are a good person, and a representative of a religion repeatedly tells you that you are "bad," is that judgment likewise an invasion of your boundaries?

Have you ever experienced having any of your other spiritual boundaries invaded? What specifically happened? Feel free to write about these here or in your journal or diary.

2

Checking My Boundaries

For a number of reasons, it may be useful to check out what my boundaries may be like now. I may have grown up in a family where healthy boundaries were neither modeled nor taught. I may have been — and may still be — in one or more relationships where I and others are unclear about boundaries and limits.

The following is a survey wherein anyone interested can check out their own personal boundaries and limits.

Table 2.1. Survey on Personal Boundaries

Circle or check the word that most applies to how you truly feel.

1. I can't make up my mind.

   Never   Seldom   Occasionally   Often   Usually

2. I have difficulty saying "no" to people.

   Never   Seldom   Occasionally   Often   Usually

3. I feel as if my happiness depends on other people.

   Never   Seldom   Occasionally   Often   Usually

4. It's hard for me to look a person in the eyes.

   Never   Seldom   Occasionally   Often   Usually

5. I find myself getting involved with people who end up hurting me.

   Never   Seldom   Occasionally   Often   Usually

6. I trust others.

   Never   Seldom   Occasionally   Often   Usually

7. I would rather attend to others than attend to myself.

   Never   Seldom   Occasionally   Often   Usually

8. Others' opinions are more important than mine.

   Never   Seldom   Occasionally   Often   Usually

9. People take or use my things without asking me.

   Never   Seldom   Occasionally   Often   Usually

10. I have difficulty asking for what I want or what I need.

    Never   Seldom   Occasionally   Often   Usually

11. I lend people money and don't seem to get it back on time.

    Never   Seldom   Occasionally   Often   Usually

12. Some people I lend money to don't ever pay me back.

    Never   Seldom   Occasionally   Often   Usually

13. I feel ashamed.

    Never   Seldom   Occasionally   Often   Usually

14. I would rather go along with another person or other people than express what I'd really like to do.

    Never   Seldom   Occasionally   Often   Usually

15. I feel bad for being so "different" from other people.

    Never   Seldom   Occasionally   Often   Usually

16. I feel anxious, scared or afraid.

    Never   Seldom   Occasionally   Often   Usually

17. I spend my time and energy helping others so much that I neglect my own wants and needs.

Never   Seldom   Occasionally   Often   Usually

18. It's hard for me to know what I believe and what I think.

Never   Seldom   Occasionally   Often   Usually

19. I feel as if my happiness depends on circumstances outside of me.

Never   Seldom   Occasionally   Often   Usually

20. I feel good.

Never   Seldom   Occasionally   Often   Usually

21. I have a hard time knowing what I really feel.

Never   Seldom   Occasionally   Often   Usually

22. I find myself getting involved with people who end up being bad for me.

Never   Seldom   Occasionally   Often   Usually

23. It's hard for me to make decisions.

Never   Seldom   Occasionally   Often   Usually

24. I get angry.

Never   Seldom   Occasionally   Often   Usually

25. I don't get to spend much time alone.

Never   Seldom   Occasionally   Often   Usually

26. I tend to take on the moods of people close to me.

Never   Seldom   Occasionally   Often   Usually

27. I have a hard time keeping a confidence or secret.

Never   Seldom   Occasionally   Often   Usually

28. I am overly sensitive to criticism.

Never   Seldom   Occasionally   Often   Usually

29. I feel hurt.

Never   Seldom   Occasionally   Often   Usually

30. I tend to stay in relationships that are hurting me.

    Never   Seldom   Occasionally   Often   Usually

31. I feel an emptiness, as if something is missing in my life.

    Never   Seldom   Occasionally   Often   Usually

32. I tend to get caught up "in the middle" of other people's problems.

    Never   Seldom   Occasionally   Often   Usually

33. When someone I'm with acts up in public, I tend to feel embarrassed.

    Never   Seldom   Occasionally   Often   Usually

34. I feel sad.

    Never   Seldom   Occasionally   Often   Usually

35. It's not easy for me to really know in my heart about my relationship with a Higher Power or God.

    Never   Seldom   Occasionally   Often   Usually

36. I prefer to rely on what others say about what I should believe and do about religious or spiritual matters.

    Never   Seldom   Occasionally   Often   Usually

37. I tend to take on or feel what others are feeling.

    Never   Seldom   Occasionally   Often   Usually

38. I put more into relationships than I get out of them.

    Never   Seldom   Occasionally   Often   Usually

39. I feel responsible for other people's feelings.

    Never   Seldom   Occasionally   Often   Usually

40. My friends or acquaintances have a hard time keeping secrets or confidences which I tell them.

    Never   Seldom   Occasionally   Often   Usually

Assessing and Scoring

In your answers to this survey, many responses of "Usually" and "Often" tend to indicate more boundary problems, distortions or issues. These may also indicate some *confusion* over boundaries and limits, often called "blurred" or "fused" boundaries.

Persons who answered all or mostly "Never" may not be aware of their boundaries. A person who has healed their True Self or Child Within and who has healthy boundaries would tend to answer "Seldom" and sometimes "Occasionally." Rare items, like number 20, would be scored in the reverse.

I describe this scoring in more detail below. If you have any questions about any of these areas and dimensions of boundaries and limits, ask your therapist, counselor, therapy group or other appropriate person — including your own Child Within.

Considering My Survey Answers Further

To explore your answers to each of the questions in the survey further, you may wish to read some of the dynamically oriented descriptions of possible experiences and answers to them in the section on *Dynamics of Selected Boundary Issues* below. Doing so will allow you to go deeper into your understanding of healthy and unhealthy boundaries and limits in your relationships and your life.

Sorting Out My Boundaries

It may be helpful now to begin to summarize areas in which you may have some boundary issues or problems. To do so, refer to your answers from the *Survey*. Underline or circle the key words or phrases to which you answered "Usually," "Often" and "Never." While some "Nevers" may not indicate a boundary issue for you, many will.

If you are uncertain, ask for feedback from safe recovering people. Also consider other areas in your life that are not included in the *Survey*, in which you may have now or in the past had any possible concern about your personal boundaries. Below is some space in which to summarize these.

As I described in Chapter 1, boundaries and limits can be subdivided into being important in the physical, mental, emotional and spiritual areas of our life. Based on your accumulated experience and knowledge, and on all of the above *Survey* information, below are some spaces in which to summarize any aspect of your life where boundaries may be an issue.

Physical Boundary Problems or Issues

Mental and **Emotional** Boundary Problems or Issues

Spiritual Boundary Problems or Issues

As any of these may come up for you in your life, consider discussing them with selected safe people, such as your therapist, counselor, therapy group, sponsor or best friend. It may also be helpful to write about what comes up for you in your diary or journal. Remember to protect and maintain your boundaries by keeping what you write in a safe place.

Dynamics of Selected Boundary Issues: Toward a Further Understanding of the Survey on Personal Boundaries

On first reading each of the following descriptions, it may be difficult for some readers to associate them with personal boundaries. For others, it may be easier to see how they concern boundaries. Feel free to honor however you feel — whatever comes up for you in your inner life — when you read them. There is no right or wrong way to react to reading this material. As you read each of the following, you may wish to refer to your answers to the *Survey On Personal Boundaries*.

Reading some of the following may be ponderous and at times may even feel overwhelming. If this happens, feel free to move on to other chapters.

1. I can't make up my mind.

People may be so bound up by the mental and emotional invasion of another or others into their sacred *inner life* (their beliefs, thoughts, feelings, decisions, choices, needs, wants and experiences) that they have difficulty differentiating which of these experiences is their own and which is coming from the other person or persons. Like a sponge, they may allow others to enter their inner life to its detriment. Their boundaries may be so loose and open that they are unable to sense and determine what their own inner life is.

If my boundaries are too loose, my True Self may not have the protection for its well-being and integrity that it needs to sense, form, *experience* and *use* these various components of its inner life. Therefore, in an unhealthy state of boundaries, a person might answer this item as "Often" or "Usually." These responses would tend to indicate that the person often can't make up their mind, and thus indicate a possible boundary issue.

(Many of the dynamics in this one are related to those in items 14, 18 and 23.)

2. I have difficulty saying "no" to people.

This is related to the "people pleaser" characteristic of unhealed adult children and co-dependents, and with their concomitant difficulty being assertive. In a need to protect the immediate feeling state of our Child Within or True Self, we may respond to someone's desires or wishes with immediate agreement, when we really are undecided or may not want to say yes. This compliance will often ease our immediate confusion or other emotional pain, since to say "No," or "I need some time to think about that," may be harder for us to express — because of that confusion or pain. We also may not have had this kind of limit-setting or boundary establishment modeled for us as children.

A boundary issue would be indicated by an "Often" or "Usually" response. A person with overly *rigid* boundaries may respond "Never" to this item and to many of the other items.

(Many of the dynamics in this one are related to those in items 14, 22, 25, 33 and 38.)

3. I feel as if my happiness depends on other people.

As I recover, I discover that no person, place or thing outside of myself can make me happy. Nothing outside of me can fill my emptiness. The only thing that will fill me and allow me to feel my happiness is to discover, be and live from and as my True Self, and then experientially connect with my Higher Power. If I believe that my happiness depends on another person, I will be giving away my power and setting myself up for living in response to their moods. I have thus lost my healthy independence and have become unhealthily dependent, i.e., co-dependent, on the other. A response on this item of "Often" or "Usually" would indicate a boundary issue or problem, wherein I am not aware of my True Self enough to experience its own inherent love, fullness and happiness.

(Many of the dynamics in this one are related to those in items 21, 28, 29, 31, 34, 36, 37 and 39.)

4. It's hard for me to look a person in the eyes.

The eyes are said to be the windows of the soul. It is as though when a person looks into my eyes they can see through me and into me, into my True Self. If I am feeling bad about my True Self, it may be hard for me to make eye contact, which would allow them to see how "bad" I really am.

A response of "Often" or "Usually" to this item tends to indicate the combination of the feeling and experience of *shame* in association with a possible boundary issue. If my True Self had its integrity and felt okay about itself, I might look others in the eyes and allow them to look back into mine and feel okay about doing that. To feel okay, I would generally need to have healthy boundaries for myself and in interacting with others.

(Many of the dynamics in this one are related to those in items 14, 15, 28 and 29.)

5. I find myself getting involved with people who end up hurting me.

My awareness of my inner life may be so low that I am unable to discern *appropriate* from *inappropriate* behavior and detect who may be hurting me in any way. If I *repeatedly* allow people to hurt me, I may not be fully aware of my True Self, and thus may not have the boundaries to protect its well-being and integrity.

An "Often" or "Usually" response, and to some extent even a response of "Occasionally," indicates the possibility of weak or unhealthy boundaries. (This one is related to the dynamics in items 14, 16, 22, 28, 30, 32, 38 and 40.)

6. I trust others.

This item is more complicated. Trust comes from my being able to know and rely upon my True Self and my inner life, to such an extent that I am able to be flexible and go with the flow of an interaction in a relationship. Knowing that my inner life will provide me with a constant monitoring system for my needs and wants, I can let go of my need to control or doubt the other, and surrender into the moment of the relationship. Because I trust myself, I trust the other. I have also been aware of the other's behavior and how I have felt with that behavior over time to such an extent that I have a fairly clear sense of whether or not I can trust the person right now.

A response of "Never," "Seldom" or "Occasionally" may indicate a boundary issue that is related to the core recovery issue of trust. In this sense, what we may not be able to trust is the inner life of our True Self. And a reason why we may not be able to trust the part of our True Self is because we have not established healthy *boundaries* to maintain its well-being and integrity. On the other hand, responses of "Often" or "Usually" may also indicate either an over-trusting of others or healthy personal boundaries, depending on who we trust and the effects of that trusting on us over time. I discuss the core recovery issue of difficulty trusting and over-trusting in my book in process, *Wisdom to Know the Difference.* [115]

(See also items 11 and 12 for similar dynamics.)

7. I would rather attend to others than attend to myself.

An "Often" or "Usually" response indicates boundaries that are too loose, and a "Never" response indicates boundaries that are too constricted. There are times when it would be healthy and self-affirming to choose to help another or others rather than myself, and this might be indicated by an answer of "Seldom" or "Occasionally." In helping or attending to another in this way we might make a conscious, fully aware choice. Or we might attend to them by pure reflex, such as in an emergency situation; here on retrospective reflection we would be fully aware that such helping or attending to another was fully appropriate for the circumstances.

Remembering that boundaries function to protect the well-being and integrity of my True Self, the boundary distortion, problem or issue here would be specifically a neglect of the inner life of my True Self. Often reflecting a low self-esteem, it says that my needs and wants are less important than those of others. When I neglect or ignore my wants and needs, my Child Within tends to go into hiding. And when it hides, it hides from *me*, from my consciousness and awareness, so that I don't fully experience what is really going on for me. I thereby lose a lot of my personal power and experience in my life. Maintaining healthy boundaries supports my personal power and full experience of life.

(Many of the dynamics in this one are related to those in items 3, 25, 33, 37, 38 and 39.)

8. Others' opinions are more important than mine.

Here an "Often" or "Usually" response indicates boundaries that are too loose, and a "Never" indicates boundaries that are too constricted. When we are fully aware of our inner life, we watch and observe what is happening there, including how people and things outside us are associated with what is coming up in our inner life. From this experience we can form authentic opinions. They are authentic because they originate within us, based on our primary experience, and not on what another tells us we have to believe or share with them.

Many adult children and co-dependents grow up with their inner life being neither recognized nor supported. And so they may have difficulty forming an opinion about anything unless it is told them by another. In childhood this other is often a parent or parent figure, although it may be any one or more of family or household members — or others outside the home. These dynamics are nearly always associated with the development of boundaries that are too loose or too rigid.

In answering "Never," I may not consider others' opinions and try to understand them. I may not try to account for their viewpoint and factor it into mine. (Many of the dynamics in this one are related to those in items 2, 3, 7, 13, 14, 17, 18, 19, 21 and 26.)

9. People take or use my things without asking me.

An "Often" or "Usually" response indicates boundaries that are too loose, and a "Never" response *may* indicate boundaries that are too tight.

As we form our sense of self, with its boundaries and limits in the many components of that self, we may form extensions that include people, places and things with which we have a close relationship. We can make understandings, agreements and contracts with selected people and we can own some places and things. When we do this, we can come to feel as if they are a part of us. We make a kind of attachment to them.

If someone invades our territory or possessions in any way, including taking them without asking us, it is in this sense an invasion of our personal boundaries. The cause of this boundary invasion may be either another person with their own boundary distortions or our boundaries being too loose, or both.

(Many of the dynamics in this one are related to those in items 5, 8, 11, 12, 22, 28 and 40.)

10. I have difficulty asking for what I want or what I need.

An "Often" or "Usually" response indicates a boundary problem. When I don't know my *needs* or *wants*, which are important parts of my *inner life*, it means that I don't know who I really am. I may not be fully aware of my True Self. To be aware of and to experience my True Self, my Child Within, I need to have a sense of my personal boundaries and limits. My boundaries and limits help me to protect and maintain the well-being and integrity of my True Self. When I live my life from and as my True Self, I am aware of my powerful inner life, which includes my wants and needs.

I am responsible for seeing that my wants and needs are met. I may do so by any of several ways, including doing them myself, asking others, asking my Higher Power or a combination of any of these.

A "Never" response may indicate an unhealthy narcissism or inability to be vulnerable, or expecting others to read my mind and thus care for me. (Many of the dynamics in this one are related to those in items 1, 2, 3, 8, 14, 18, 21, 23, 26, 33, 37 and 39.)

11. I lend people money and don't seem to get it back on time.

A response of "Often" or "Occasionally" indicates a boundary problem. Related to item numbers 5, 6, 9, 12, 22 and 30, this one suggests that we may not have been clear in our agreement with another, or that we pick unreliable people to lend money to, or both. Since money is a possession, if you haven't read the explanation for item 9 above, it may be helpful to do so. Many of its principles may apply here.

12. Some people I lend money to don't ever pay me back.

Perhaps a response of "Occasionally" and certainly one of "Often" or "Usually" indicates a boundary problem. This is a more extreme example of the problems and dynamics described in item 11 above.

13. I feel ashamed.

A response of "Often" or "Usually" indicates a boundary problem, and a "Never" response may indicate a lack of awareness of feelings. In some, a "Seldom" or "Occasionally" may also be associated with an advanced state of healing and recovery.

As I described the feeling of shame in *Healing the Child Within* and describe it further in *Feelings*, it is a painful feeling that we adult children and co-dependents experience frequently growing up. And it usually continues on into adulthood. It is only when we reach a moderate to advanced stage of recovery that we may have a substantial decrease in the intensity and frequency of feeling shame. By that time we are clearly and fully aware of what shame is.

Nearly all shame is unnecessary. It serves no useful purpose. What shame suggests is that we are somehow bad, inadequate or not enough. In recovery we learn that we are a good, whole and perfect child of God. And how could something that is part of God be bad or defective? So when another, whether our parent, a parent figure or *anyone* — including religious leaders or teachers — indicates to us in *any way* that we are inadequate, bad or a "sinner," they are invading our personal boundaries. They are trying to violate our personal integrity. And if we feel that shame, and certainly if we hold on to it, we are *letting* them invade our boundaries.

(Many of the dynamics in this one are related to those in items 3, 4, 10, 13, 15, 17, 18, 21, 22, 30, 31 and 33.)

14. I would rather go along with another person or other people than express what I'd really like to do.

If I don't know what I would like to do on an occasion, whether it be going to a certain movie or event, staying home or doing any other activity, I may not be fully aware of my inner life. And if I'm not fully aware of my inner life, my True Self — my Child Within — may have gone into hiding. The absence of healthy boundaries may be one reason why our Child Within goes into hiding. Our pain becomes too much.

On the opposite end, if my boundaries are too rigid and tight, I may experience a frequent or consistent difficulty being flexible enough to do or participate in what a close or intimate person or what a group of others prefers to do. This would be important mostly if my rigidity caused repeated conflicts with a person or people whom I valued in having an ongoing relationship.

A response of "Occasionally," "Often" or "Usually" indicates a boundary problem, nearly always one of having boundaries that are too loose. A response of "Never" or "Seldom" generally indicates either healthy boundaries or overly rigid boundaries.

(Most of the principles described in items 1, 2, 4, 10 and 23 will apply here, so it may be helpful to review those if you like.)

15. I feel bad for being so "different" from other people.

In recovery we learn that each of us is a *unique* child of God. Why would God make things different? Rocks, animals, fingerprints, people — each one similar in its group, yet also different and unique. The boundaries that our True Self creates around itself maintain the well-being, inner life, integrity, creativity and personal power that it generates. While each of these characteristics is similar, or at times even the same as others', each is also different and unique.

It is in aspects of *both* our uniqueness and our sameness that our personal power lies. We have a right to know and use our personal power, which our boundaries and limits help us maintain.

A response of "Occasionally," "Often" or "Usually" indicates a boundary problem. A response of "Seldom" or "Never" may indicate either healthy boundaries or a lack of awareness about feelings.

Similar to items 4, 13 and 33, this one also reflects a feeling of shame for being who I am, and perhaps for my physical appearance or other aspects of myself.

I realize that this chapter contains concentrated reading in these descriptions. Feel free to move on to other chapters or take a break from it whenever you like.

16. I feel anxious, scared or afraid.

Boundaries that are too loose may be indicated here by answers of "Often" or "Usually."

When we feel fear, we may be letting our boundaries be invaded. Someone may have threatened us in some way, such as with some form of mistreatment or by choosing to leave or abandon us in some way. Or we may be about to lose some of our money or a possession. Or perhaps we are actually being mistreated or abandoned or losing something. And that hurts. When that happens or is about to happen, we can feel all kinds of pain, including fear.

But when we experientially learn who we really are — our True Self, our Child Within — and eventually experientially learn of its connection to our Higher Power, we discover that even though we may have to grieve such a loss, no one can ever abandon us or destroy us. We are already and always a precious Child of God, always connected and protected by that God. We are safe, absolutely safe. At all times.

I am going to make perhaps a seemingly outrageous state- ment about fear. Nearly every time that we feel fear in any form, we are letting our personal boundaries be invaded in some fashion. As I describe in *Feelings* and *Wisdom to Know the Difference*, fear is an almost totally unnecessary feeling. In all practicality, it has almost no usefulness. This is a tough one to sort out. Certainly there are emergency situations when fear may have some degree of usefulness. But in most situa- tions, and certainly from a higher and spiritual perspective, it is not useful.

We either create fear (most of it), it is inflicted upon us (some of it) or both (a lot of it). But we don't need to suffer from it unless we let it or someone or some thought invade our boundaries. The most common one to invade our bound- aries is our ego, specifically our negative ego or co-dependent self, which thrives on fear. Whether we feel panic, are "walk- ing on eggs" or feel a little bit afraid, we will usually be giving in to our false self running our life at that instant.

So what we can do is to feel the fear, recognize it, identify it, and decide whether it has any usefulness at all for us at that moment. Nearly always it will not. So we can then let go of it. With practice it often will disappear. I describe fear in more detail in my recorded talks on feelings and a separate talk on fear itself, available from Perrin & Treggett.[110]

(Many of the dynamics in this one are related to those in item 2.)

17. I spend my time and energy helping others so much that I neglect my own wants and needs.

An answer of "Often," "Usually" or "Never" here indicates a boundary problem.

Boundaries and limits protect the integrity and well-being of our True Self. If we neglect our True Self, not only does it suffer the consequences of that neglect, but the neglect may also render it more susceptible to the invasion of its boundaries by people, places and things, some of which may be unsafe for us.

So it is important that we tend to our wants and needs. Doing so will both maintain our well-being and help protect us from inappropriate invasion of the sacred, vulnerable and powerful inner life of our True Self.

18. It's hard for me to know what I believe and what I think.

An answer of "Often," "Usually" or "Never" indicates a boundary problem.

Occasionally it is healthy and appropriate to be confused or not know exactly what I believe or think. These may be times when new input and information is coming into me. Before I make a decision, I need some time to think in various ways about it and to consider various possibilities.

So it is healthy to feel confused at times. Anyone who isn't confused *at times* isn't in recovery, i.e., they may be denying or not aware of sometimes feeling confused. But when we are confused so often that we frequently don't know what we believe or think, some person, place or thing may be invading our personal boundaries. (This question and these dynamics may be related to those in items 1, 10, 21, 23, 32 and 36.)

19. I feel as if my happiness depends on circumstances outside of me.

Responses of "Often" and "Usually" indicate a boundary problem.

Ultimately, my happiness or fulfillment depends on knowing and living from and as who I really am — my True Self — and then connecting that in a healthy way to my Higher Power and safe others. When I don't live in this way, I am living inauthentically, as a false self, which usually produces emptiness and unhappiness. My false self cannot give me lasting happiness or fulfillment. The only way the false self can produce a brief glimpse of fulfillment is by looking outside of itself. It looks at people, places, things, behaviors and experiences for the answer.

When my True Self is in hiding, it may not have appropriate boundaries and limits to protect itself — to maintain its well-being and integrity so that it can stay out, fully in its consciousness. (See also numbers 8, 20, 26 and 31.)

20. I feel good.

Answers of "Never," "Seldom" or "Occasionally" indicate a boundary problem.

This item is related to number 19 above, with feeling good being equivalent to feeling happy. The only part of us that can feel happy, fulfilled and good is our True Self. And the only way that our True Self can feel so in a *lasting* way is eventually to connect with the God of our understanding.

21. I have a hard time knowing what I really feel.

A response of "Often" or "Usually" indicates a boundary problem. We cannot know our real feelings without living as our True Self, being aware of our crucial inner life — of which our feelings are a major part — and we protect our inner life with healthy boundaries.

(This item is related to the dynamics described in numbers 19 and 20 above, as well as those in numbers 3, 13, 24, 26, 31, 37 and 39.)

22. I find myself getting involved with people who end up being bad for me.

Since boundaries and limits protect the well-being and integrity of my True Self, when I repeatedly get involved with people who hurt me, I am likely not to be fully aware of and using my personal boundaries and limits.

A response of "Often" or "Usually" indicates a boundary problem. (This one is related to items 2, 5, 9, 11, 12, 14, 38 and 40.)

23. It's hard for me to make decisions.

When my True Self is in hiding (Figure 4.2 on page 57), it may be hard to know all of what is going on in my inner life. To make healthy decisions, I need to know what is going on in my inner life, including my beliefs, thoughts, feelings, choices, intuitions and all other experiences that I may be aware of. Each of these is usually a factor when I make a decision. As described throughout this book, my personal boundaries and limits help protect the well-being and integrity of my True Self so that it doesn't have to remain in hiding.

An answer of "Often" or "Usually" indicates a boundary problem. (This one is related to the dynamics described in items 1, 10, 18 and 21.)

24. I get angry.

To help us establish appropriate and healthy boundaries and limits is one of the few ways that getting angry can be of any usefulness to us, as I describe in Chapter 11. Getting angry can give us the *energy* and *motivation* to set the boundary or limit.

An answer of "Never," "Often" or "Usually" indicates a boundary problem.

(This one is related to the dynamics described in item 21 above and in the others to which number 21 is related.)

25. I don't get to spend much time alone.

An answer of "Often" or "Usually" indicates a problem with boundaries.

We heal our True Self and live a healthy and fulfilled life in three relationships: with our self alone, with safe others and, if we choose, with our Higher Power. We need an appropriate time alone to question, consider, reflect, contemplate, meditate, rest, renew and just be. Spending such time alone and aware gives us the space to do these. It also helps us get our needs met.

Without healthy boundaries and limits, it can be difficult to spend enough time alone for these crucial activities *and inactivities*. If we are around others a lot, and if others make many demands on us so that we cannot spend enough time alone, we can create time alone by setting healthy boundaries and limits and by asking for what we want and need.

(This one is related to items numbers 2, 7, 10, 14 and 17 above.)

26. I tend to take on the moods of people close to me.

We tend to learn boundaries and limits — or a lack of them — from a young age in our family of origin. While doing so can be a survival technique, it is usually directly taught to us, and so it is not our fault that we learned unhealthy and blurred boundaries. However, once we begin to heal ourselves and set healthy boundaries and limits, we discover that we no longer need to take on the moods or feelings of others. This then leaves us free to feel healthy empathy and compassion for others, without needing to feel responsible for their feelings or to fix them. (See also discussion in the Appendix.)

An answer of "Often" or "Usually" indicates a boundary problem. (This one is related to many of the dynamics in items number 19, 21, 32, 37 and 39. If you haven't read them, it may be useful to review items 19 and 21.)

27. I have a hard time keeping a confidence or a healthy secret.

A response of "Occasionally," "Often" or "Usually" indicates a boundary problem. As background for this item, please see my brief introduction to *secrets* in *A Gift to Myself*. Here it is helpful to differentiate a confidence or a healthy secret, where neither you nor any other person is harmed by keeping it, and a toxic secret where you and/or another may be harmed by keeping the confidence.

Unhealed adult children and co-dependent people often feel as if they either have to "tell all" or "keep it all inside," in an all-or-none fashion. In recovery we learn that we never have to tell another person *anything* about ourself or our relationship with another. We always have choices about what we can tell or not tell, say or not say, in any conversation or communication.

A useful question is, "Will telling a secret harm me or any other? Will it harm the integrity of my True Self or will it harm another or hurt their feelings in any way?" Another is, "Whose business is it to know this information anyway?" This concept is also reflected in the Ninth Step: "Made direct amends to those we had harmed wherever possible, *except where to do so would injure them or others.*"

Healthy boundaries and limits help us to maintain our own integrity and well-being, as well as those of others when appropriate. (This item is related to number 40 below.)

28. I am overly sensitive to criticism.

If someone criticizes me, the first thing I feel is an invasion of my boundaries. I may even age regress and feel like a helpless little child. (See Chapter 5 on age regression.) Once I recover from that, I have to determine if their criticism is valid. If it is, I may feel fear of change and more painfully, shame over the mistake — and then grieving the loss, and finally letting go of it.

Usually the statement, "What others think of me is none of my business" applies here.[108] While we are still accountable for what we say and do, once we live from and as our True Self and then connect to our Higher Power, we can have the awareness and confidence that we are absolutely fine the way we are. As we heal, we learn experientially what fear and shame are, and in our advanced recovery we learn to let go of them. In fact, these two painful feelings are nearly always unnecessary. Yet without awareness and boundaries, we can let fear and shame stifle and at times paralyze our peace, joy and creativity. These latter three are what *A Course in Miracles* says is God's will for us.[25]

A response of "Occasionally," "Often" or "Usually" indicates a boundary problem. A response of "Never" may reflect a lack of awareness of a person's inner life, and thus perhaps overly rigid boundaries. (This one is related to some of the dynamics described in items 3, 4, 13, 15, 16, 29, 33 and 39.)

29. I feel hurt.

If we often or usually feel hurt, it is likely that we are either letting others invade our personal boundaries, we are ourselves creating our hurt, or both. A major source for creating hurt and other painful feelings in ourself is having grown up in a dysfunctional or unhealthy family or other environment, with all its dynamics, including giving ourself the negative and painful messages we so often received. And we may still be in an unhealthy environment. Without healthy boundaries and limits, we can continue to be mistreated and continue to repeat to ourselves the painful messages.

When we create healthy boundaries and limits for ourselves, we protect the well-being and integrity of our Child Within, our True Self. And this means that we will not feel emotional pain or hurt unnecessarily.

At times it is appropriate and necessary that we experience and work through some painful feelings. Doing so is a healthy part of our recovery and our life. We experience and work through these feelings, and when we are complete with them, we let them go. I discuss this further in *A Gift to Myself*, *Healing the Child Within* and *Feelings*.

An answer of "Often" or "Usually" indicates a boundary problem. One of "Never" may reflect a lack of awareness of a person's inner life, and thus perhaps overly rigid boundaries. (This one is also related to the dynamics described in items 3, 4, 13, 15, 16, 28, 33 and 39.)

30. I tend to stay in relationships that are hurting me.

If I stay in a relationship that continues to hurt me, I may not be fully aware of my crucial inner life and thus of my True Self. To progress in my awareness, I will need healthy boundaries and limits to protect the well-being and integrity of my Child Within so that it will feel safe enough to come out of hiding and stay out so it can rediscover itself and heal.

Another factor is that I may have unconsciously chosen this relationship that is hurting me in an attempt to work through some unfinished business from a past relationship. One of the reasons why this business is unfinished may be due to my never learning and forming healthy boundaries and limits in the first place. Thus, while painful, this relationship may be an opportunity to experience, learn and grow in my healing.

An answer of "Occasionally," "Often" or "Usually" indicates a boundary problem. An answer of "Never" may indicate either overly rigid boundaries or an advanced state of healing and being. (This one is related to the dynamics described in items 5, 14, 16, 22, 32, 38 and 40.)

31. I feel an emptiness, as if something is missing in my life.

It is my personal and clinical experience that what most often causes the painful feeling of emptiness is the absence of our full awareness of our True Self or Child Within. Our Child goes into hiding, and we just feel empty. Healthy boundaries and limits help us protect the integrity and well-being of our Child Within. When it feels protected, it feels safe. And when it feels safe, it can come out and stay out to explore, experience, connect, create, celebrate and be. It feels alive and fulfilled. The emptiness begins to disappear slowly.

When our Child Within or True Self experientially connects with its Higher Power by feeling its unconditional love, it is eventually progressively so fulfilled that the emptiness goes away. We no longer need to fill our emptiness with people, places and things from the outside. This experience then frees us to relate to selected, safe and appropriate people, places and things in a healthy way.

An answer of "Occasionally," "Often" or "Usually" may indicate a lack of healthy boundaries and limits. An answer of "Never" may indicate a lack of awareness of inner life *or* possible complete healing, including self-realization and realization of my Higher Power. (This one is related to many of the dynamics in items 3, 13, 17, 19, 20, 21 and 35.)

32. I tend to get caught up "in the middle" of other people's problems.

Here my boundary problem may occur in one or both of two ways: I let others invade my boundaries and/or I invade others' boundaries inappropriately. Others may involve me in their problems by the former, if I let them, and I may get myself involved inappropriately in others' business or problems by the latter. This process may be related to several *core recovery issues*, such as control, over-responsibility for others, feelings, all-or-none thinking and behaving, fear of abandonment, low self-esteem and shame, high tolerance for inappropriate behavior and difficulty being real or authentic. (See also Chapters 11 & 12 on core issues.)

These core issues and this process are also related to the dynamics of feeling empty and trying to fill our emptiness by getting caught up in the middle of other people's problems (see also items 3 and 31 above). This dynamic can occur with most anyone, covers a spectrum from a little involvement or a lot, and may be subtle or overt. An example of subtle involvement may be a helping professional who cannot remain objective with a patient or client and gets more involved than is necessary to help the person, which could result in hurting either or both of them. (See also Chapters 13 & 14 on triangles.)

Of course, there are times when getting involved and helping another are appropriate and healthy, not harmful, and would thus not constitute a boundary problem in either direction. Examples are when another *asks us* for assistance and we go only as far as they ask, and when we offer to assist another from an attitude of unconditional giving or love.

A response of "Occasionally," "Often" or "Usually" indicates a problem with boundaries. (This one is related to the dynamics in items 5, 17, 18, 26, 27, 30 and 37.)

33. When someone I'm with acts up in public, I tend to feel embarrassed.

Related to several core issues, especially difficulty being real, feelings, low self-esteem, shame and over-responsibility for others, becoming embarrassed (feeling ashamed in the presence of more than one person) when another acts a certain way or acts up is usually an indication of boundaries that are too loose, or possibly enmeshment with the others in our presence.

An answer of "Often" or "Usually" indicates a boundary problem, and one of "Occasionally" may also, depending on the circumstances. A response of "Never" may indicate a lack of awareness of our inner life or a possible complete healing, including having healthy boundaries. (This one is related to the dynamics in items number 2, 7, 10, 14, 17, 21, 26, 31, 32, 37 and 39.)

34. I feel sad.

When we have a loss, it is appropriate through our healthy grieving process to feel sad for a while. Healthy grieving usually indicates the presence of healthy boundaries. However, when we are often or usually sad without clear and appropriately recent losses or traumas, it may indicate that we have not grieved important losses in our past. Such experience frequently indicates the presence of unhealthy boundaries. This is because we grieve in healthier ways as our boundaries become healthier.

Our True Self is the being that grieves. Since healthy boundaries protect and maintain the well-being and integrity of our True Self — so that it can stay out of hiding and experience and be — with them we are free to react in any spontaneous and healthy way, including grieving. So chronic sadness usually indicates ungrieved grief and thus a boundary problem.

A response of "Often" or "Usually" frequently indicates a boundary problem, and a response of "Never" may indicate a lack of awareness of our inner life. (This one is related to the dynamics in items number 2, 19 and 29.)

35. It's not easy for me to really know in my heart about my relationship with a Higher Power or God.

An answer of "Often" or "Usually" indicates a boundary problem, and one of "Occasionally" is a borderline indicator of a boundary problem.

Knowing in my heart means that my Child Within or True Self knows in an experiential or felt way. To feel the presence of God in my heart requires that I experientially know my heart, my True Self, well enough so I can loosen my boundaries enough to allow the love, wisdom and healing power of God to come in.

To so loosen my boundaries, I need to have healthy ones to begin with so that my heart can feel protected and safe enough to open to my Higher Power. It is contradictory that many people's experiences with organized religions that tend to induce shame, guilt and fear may close their hearts and send their Child Within into hiding to such an extent that they are unable to open their hearts to the God of their understanding. They are thus unable to be whole and feel fulfilled. I and others believe that this behavior by clergy or others in the name of any religion is mistreatment and abuse. (See also item numbers 3 and 31 above for related dynamics.)

36. I tend to rely on what others say about what I should believe and do about religious or spiritual matters.

While families and cultures, including religions themselves, may give advice, suggestions and at times directives or proclamations about what we "should" believe or do religiously or spiritually, it appears that the only way we can have an authentic religious or spiritual experience is from a felt sense in our own heart and soul. To have such an authentic experience, we usually need to have a free Child Within, one that is not in hiding. To be so free, we need healthy boundaries. This one is similar to the dynamics in many of the other items above, including numbers 3, 31 and 35.

An answer of "Often" or "Usually" indicates a boundary problem, with one of "Occasionally" possibly indicating a boundary problem. An answer of "Never" could also indicate a boundary problem.

37. I tend to take on or feel what others are feeling.

This one is nearly identical with the scoring and dynamics in item number 26 above. (Its dynamics are similar to many of the above, especially numbers 3, 7, 10, 17, 21, 28, 29, 30 through 33 and 39.)

38. I put more into relationships than I get out of them.

If I tend more to others' needs and neglect my own, this indicates that I have weak or unhealthy boundaries. This may be manifested by such dynamics and behaviors as spending more energy on the relationship than the others do, pursuing them more (see also "Pursuing versus Distancing" in Chapter 10), and giving anything such as gifts, time or other things to the other more than they may tend to give to me. Part of what is healthy and missing here is *mutuality*, a sense of equality in sharing of interest, energy and time.

An answer of "Often," "Usually" or "Never" indicates a boundary problem. (Many of its dynamics are related to those in items number 2, 5, 7, 14, 17, 22, 30 and 32 above.)

39. I feel responsible for other people's feelings.

As described in item 33 above and in the others listed, this one is related to the core issue of over-responsibility for others and the basic dynamics of bonding versus bondage and healthy boundaries and limits versus enmeshment. (See Chapters 7, 8 and 9.) It is also related to the experiences of true compassion versus passion.

A response of "Often" or "Usually" indicates a boundary problem. An answer of "Never" could also indicate a boundary problem, depending on individual circumstances. (Many of the dynamics of this one are related to those in items number 3, 7, 10, 14, 17, 26, 31, 32, 33 and 37.)

40. My friends or acquaintances have a hard time keeping secrets or confidences which I tell them.

A response of "Occasionally," "Often" or "Usually" indicates a boundary problem.

(The dynamics described under item number 27 above apply to this one.)

Conclusion

While it may be ponderous and at times even boring to read these descriptions above, doing so can help with both a better understanding of some of the dynamics of boundaries and limits and a more effective use of the *Survey on Personal Boundaries*.

If you get bogged down or stuck while reading this or the next two chapters, consider moving on to Chapter 5.

3

A History Of Boundaries

The idea of boundaries is not new. We are just rediscovering them now and developing clearer and healthier ideas and practices from and about them, as we are doing with many dynamics and issues.

To understand how boundaries have evolved into our present-day conceptions, we can take a brief look at them over the ages as they relate to our True Self, as outlined in Figure 3.1 below.

About 2,500 years ago the Buddha began to describe aspects of the individual self, as did Lao-tzu in the *Tao te Ching*, referring to its outside attachments as the "10,000 things." [19,57a] These descriptions of our "individual self" addressed aspects of a part of our psyche or mind that is commonly referred to today as "ego." From Jesus' time the New Testament translators called it the "self." What he modeled and taught was *living* his True Self, his Child Within: "To get into the Kingdom of Heaven, you have to become like a little child" (Matthew 18:3). He also addressed boundaries, e.g.,

"Don't build your house on loose ground," (Matthew 7:26) and "Don't cast your pearls among swine" (Matthew 7:6).

Although more technical, in the early 1900s Freud wasn't as clear as Christ in differentiating the True Self from the ego self. Indeed, he appears, perhaps unawares, to have combined these two parts of our psyche into one concept — "ego" — as did Carl Jung and others.

It was not until the 1930s, when Hartmann described the *ego ideal* and when Horney, Klein, Winnicott and others coined the term *real* or *true self*, that we began once again to differentiate the ego self from the True Self.[41,47,81] And continuing even to today, therapists and theorists in object relations and self-psychology appropriately separate the two — true self and false self, i.e., ego.[56,73]

Figure 3.1. Evolution of Our Understanding of the True Self
(Reading from left to right)

This figure shows a progressively clearer differentiation between the True Self and false self over the past 2,500 years, ending with a simplified version of my "map" of the psyche (realizing that "the map is not the territory"). In this map, the True Self (Child Within) is in relationship with its Higher Self and Higher Power, and the false self or ego is simply an assistant to the True Self. Boundaries are helpful in maintaining this differentiation.

Current Views

Modern psychology theory and practice thus now clearly differentiates between the self, which I call the True Self, and the ego as being two separate but related parts of our psyche. In this understanding, the *True Self* is the being, consciousness and essence that we really are, and *ego* or false self is our assistant which helps us deal with the world.[109]

However, most of the earlier writings about boundaries over the past 100 years still use the older *combined* and often confusing term for both True Self and ego as "ego," and thus frequently refer to the term "ego boundary." Based on our modern understanding of the True Self as being *separate* from the false self or ego, it is now more accurate to think of boundary as being a *creative dynamic of the True Self* or self, since the True Self makes and uses healthy boundaries to protect and maintain its integrity and well-being.

Thus, in this expanded view, the ego has little to do with healthy boundaries. True Self makes and maintains its own healthy boundaries, while the false self or ego can't and doesn't.

What ego can do and does, however, is to make unhealthy boundaries as walls of separation between us and other people, places and things,[25,110] and it may even distort or blur our attempts at forming healthy boundaries. A more accurate and useful term than "ego boundary" today is thus *self boundary*. That creative, maintaining and flexible dynamic — boundary — is what I am describing throughout this book.

But how else have clinicians, teachers and writers viewed boundaries through the ages? In the sections below, I describe an overview of some ancient and modern views of boundaries.

Some Ancient Views on Boundaries

In ancient times, spiritual masters, teachers and philosophers spoke of boundaries in various ways throughout their writings. For example, around 500 B.C. the Buddha lived and taught a path of wakefulness, observation and detachment. What we are awake to and what we observe is our *inner life,* and we learn to detach from its unnecessary pain. One of the ways that we detach is by being aware of boundaries, as the Buddha wrote:

> *An unreflecting mind is a poor roof.*
> *Passion, like the rain, floods the house.*
> *But if the roof is strong, there is shelter.*

Here he speaks of the roof as a boundary. Another way that he describes boundary is:

> *By watching and working*
> *The master makes for himself an island*
> *Which the flood cannot overwhelm.*
>
> Dhammapada, c. 500-200 BC[19]

While we can consider and discuss the possible meanings of these lines at length, they give us but one example of how boundaries have been important in our survival for millennia.

Table 3.1. Some Ancient Historical Perspectives of Boundaries

---

Buddha (c. 500 BC) — importance of detachment from individual self (ego, co-dependent self) and unnecessary pain.

Lao-tzu (c. 500 BC) — importance of nonattachment to the "10,000 things," which Twelve-Step workers also call "people, places and things."

Jesus Christ — importance of living life as true self, connected to God and fellow humans. He also taught that while you can accept, forgive and love those who are not truly God-minded and who hurt you, you do not have to stay around them and let them mistreat you.

Boundary and the Metaphor of Magic

In legends and myths, the process of self-transformation and recovery has been described in various ways. One of these has been by using the word "magic." In these stories, which we can use to reflect aspects of our struggle with the human condition (what we now can call co-dependence), magic is a word we can use to describe what we do when we risk being real, as we recover and live our lives more fully. This kind of magic is not sleight-of-hand or "black magic." Rather, it is the hard work of healing our True Self. When a magician wants to work magic, the story goes, he puts a circle around himself (Figure 3.2). It is within this bounded circle, this hermetically sealed-off area, that powers can be brought into play which are lost outside the circle.

**Figure 3.2. The Magician as a Metaphor for the
Self-Actualized or Recovered Person**
(from Campbell J: The Power of Myth p.215)

Gray says, "To an outside observer ignorant of the process, few things might seem more ridiculous than an adult person making rings around themselves and attaching mental labels at the intersections like some childish game. In fact, however, the principles behind the practice are as sound and scientific on spiritual levels as any form of designing on physical ones. . . . Naturally, the individual ability of the operator is a decisive factor, upon which the efficacious degree of any circle depends."[39] Who is the magician? Who is the hero in these myths and legends? It is us. We are the magician, the hero and the heroine, as we live out the Divine Mystery. And it is by making, maintaining or letting go of and using healthy boundaries that our True Self can dare to come out of hiding.

But throughout history some institutions, such as organized religion, have often confused us about healthy boundaries. Sometimes they helped — and sometimes they were harmful. How might we tell the difference?

Boundary and Organized Religion

World religions have made commandments, guidelines and rules for living a religious life that acted as various forms of boundaries and limits. When practiced, these were to serve as protecting the faithful from "evil," which each religion attempted to define in its own way. Some of these boundaries as directives or admonitions had some usefulness, such as "Thou shall not kill." Others were often vague and confusing, such as "Honor your father and mother . . . "[78] and "Don't sin," with each religion attempting to define "sin" for us. These and other boundaries brought about individual alienation and unnecessary pain and suffering. An example is the idea of the mind and soul being separate from the body — including the sexuality and enjoyment that healthy relationships with self and others might bring, which clergy often referred to as "sin."

Over the centuries clergy in these religious systems, as well as philosophers and others, have addressed and wrestled with boundaries and limits in numerous ways. A problem is that it was difficult to sort out which of these guidelines were true and therefore useful and which were not. My sense is that each of us has to assess and sort these out in our own way and in our own time. And we can do the same for the following recent perspectives on boundaries.

Recent Historical Perspectives

With the beginning of modern psychology in the late 19th century, we continued exploring boundaries and limits, and we began to widen our understanding of them. In 1983 Polster reviewed some 15 contributions about boundaries from others and added her own.[90] I have summarized these and have added several additional ones in Table 3.2.

Early in this recent history of boundaries, writers began to describe our self-awareness and the importance of differentiating characteristics between self and others. They described the earliest aspects of boundary as being firm or flexible, solid or permeable. And Reich explored perhaps the first instance of healthy and unhealthy boundaries in his description of character armor.

Later, other clinicians and writers, describing their observations of infant and child development, hinted at and gave us a stronger developmental basis for our current understanding of boundaries, which I describe in the next chapter. Around this time also came the related fields of object relations and self psychology, which began giving us a more sophisticated, though sometimes confusing (due to some of the jargon), view of self and object (the other person), experiences and dynamics. Still later came the importance of boundaries in all relationships, including how coming to know and be our True Self was necessary before we could open our boundaries to others in having successful and enjoyable relationships.

Since the 1950s the family therapy movement has reintroduced boundaries to therapists, as did the self-help fellowship of Al-Anon, by the concept of *detachment* for many other people. More recently, the adult child and co-dependence movement has expanded all of the above, demystifying it for everyone. And over the coming years, as we each risk and heal in our own recovery, we will likely learn even more.

Table 3.2. Some Recent Historical Perspectives on Boundaries
(compiled in part from Polster, 1983)

Royce 1895 — self-consciousness, awareness of difference between self and other; product of relationships

Freud 1911 — special function to deal with external reality as infant moves from pleasure to reality principle

Ferenczi 1913 — appreciation of distinctions between self and outside world

Tausk 1933 — "ego" boundary, metaphor for consistent awareness of being separate from non-self

Lewin 1935, 1936 — boundary as solid or permeable — depending on context, relationship and systemic interaction

Reich 1949 — boundaries as character armor in rigid personality

Federn 1952 — boundary between "ego" [self] and external world and unconscious material; metaphor for a dynamic and constantly changing relationship

Rapaport 1958 — "ego's" (i.e., self's) autonomy from id and external reality

Mahler 1958 — infant's development from undifferentiated to more differentiated

Rapaport and Gill 1959 — boundary from concrete to symbolic

Erikson 1963 — further description of human development by stages

Jacobson 1964 — development of and differentiation between self- and object-representations (internalization of experienced relationships)

Searles 1965 — the ability to distinguish self from environment is part of a healthy personality; lack of boundaries at times may be useful and healthy

Wilder; Bateson 1972 — boundary as condition of all communication and locus of all relationships. Began describing primitive aspects of all-or-none thinking and behaving

Schafer 1976 — need for new language in psychoanalysis to help person be more independent and less a victim

Minuchin 1974 — boundary as a crucial dynamic in individual and family illness and health

Polster 1983 (review article) — identity differentiation and maintenance come before receptive aspect of boundary[90]

4

Boundaries And Human Development

One of the most useful ways to understand the formation of both healthy and unhealthy boundaries is from the perspective of human growth and development.

While Chapter 3 showed a few aspects of these developmental milestones (in Table 3.2 on some historical events in our understanding of boundaries), I will now describe a more detailed developmental approach in Table 4.1. In this table I correlate boundaries with tasks in human development and the approximate age around which each commonly occurs in a healthy family (left column) and in an unhealthy family (right column). This information is taken from numerous sources[20,30,60,66,112] and can be summarized as follows.

Development in a Healthy Family

Infancy and Early Childhood

Before birth, in the mother's womb, the child has no physical boundary from its mother. While this intrauterine experience remains a mystery, the developing fetus may also

Table 4.1. Tasks in Human Development and Formation of Healthy and Unhealthy Boundaries (Reading from bottom to top) (compiled in part from references 20,30,60,66,112)

Development of Healthy Boundaries of Relationships	Tasks*	Approximate Age in First Cycle	Realm of Being	Development of UNHEALTHY Boundaries & Relationships	Stage in Recovery
• Continued search for self and God • Recycle many of below	Be Co-create Extend love Transcend ego Self-realize	Later in life, usually second half, when have a sense of self that can let go of its ego	Spiritual	• Continued search for self & God • Possibility for adult child healing, including working through healthy developmental tasks & boundaries • Recycle most of below	3
• Explores intimate relationships	Recycle	19		• Dysfunctional attempts at intimate relationships	
• Struggle for further self-identity			Emotional	• Continued distorted boundaries and sense of self	
• Begins to separate from parents and family	Evolve & grow	13		• Unhealthy separation from parents and family	
• Continues developing healthy social roles	Regenerate (heal)			• Social roles to detriment of self	
• Continues exploring, with a growing sense of self	Evaluate Develop morals, skills & values Create (make)	6		• Parents, parent figures, & others continue to stifle the child's healthy exploring and self-esteem	
• Continues learning how is same and different from others	Master	4		• Distortion of sameness into co-dependence and differentness into low self-esteem	2

Healthy (A)	Task		Category	Unhealthy	
• Models behaving and thinking after parents and close others	Cooperate	3			
• Parents begin to let go of (A) below, allowing child to individuate	Think		Mental	• Unhealthy boundaries are solidified by parent's modeling and demanding boundaries to be rigid and/or too loose	1
• Begins to test limits	Separate	2			
• Still older begins to realize is separate from parents and begins to explore the world in more depth	Initiate / Explore			• Wounded themselves, parents disallow child to separate and explore for itself	
• Mother-infant symbiosis helps infant organize perceptions & feelings in a healthy giving & receiving similar to a sort of "healthy projective identification" (A)	Trust / Feel	1	Physical	• Narcissistic or otherwise distracted parents mistreat and mold infant to be an extension of their wants and needs. Parents may also neglect children causing an insecure, fragile environment	0
• Older infant believes is an extension of parents	Love / Connect			• Same as healthy	
• Infant believes is a part of and is fused with parents. Parents begin to "mirror" (see A above).	Be	0		• Same as healthy	

• We recycle throughout these tasks regularly throughout our life. Healthy adolescents repeat the first 14 to 16 tasks. Parents usually cycle in parallel with their children.

feel a oneness with God. But at birth, it is suddenly expelled, with perhaps a feeling of rejection by both its mother and God. There is immediately an open space, a sort of boundary, interjected in between. The pain of this forced separation may hurt the just-born infant so much that it could be afraid of engaging in some future relationships.

Nonetheless, in the first few months of life the infant usually experiences that it is a part of and is mentally and emotionally fused with its parents or parent figure. This experience is enforced by the parent's mirroring, which consists of the parent reflecting back to the infant in expression, posture and sounds what the parent senses that the infant is experiencing.

It is during this early time that all-or-none (splitting), good or bad, is first learned.[55,81] As it grows, the infant still believes that it is an extension of its parents, but eventually it begins to sense the earliest indications that it is separate from them, and it begins to explore.

As the child learns to separate and walk, it begins to learn that not everything is all-or-none, good or bad. Rather, it learns that some things may be both good and bad, such as walking away from the parent. In this "rapprochement" phase, it learns more about self, primitive boundaries and limits, and something about dependence and independence.[41,56,20,55,66,81,122] Still later, as a toddler, it begins to test the limits of self, others and the world, and by age four learns to model its behaving and thinking after parents and close others.

Ideally, as these early developmental experiences and events unfold, the child constructs a healthy sense of self. And an integral and crucial part of that self development is the formation and maintenance of healthy boundaries and limits. The child learns both of these — self sense and boundaries — earliest from its family of origin and later from people outside of its family. If its family of origin and environment are unhealthy, through the process of teaching and modeling, the child will learn and develop an unhealthy sense of self and unhealthy boundaries. These two tend to go together.

Latency Age

During this time, between ages 5 and 11 or 12, the child continues learning how it is similar to and different from others, which is crucial in forming boundaries. It continues exploring various aspects of itself and continues growing, not only in the physical, mental, and emotional realms, but also in the spiritual.[46] Finally, it continues developing social roles and guidelines.

Adolescence

By adolescence the person again begins to separate from its parents and family. It is here that the parents need to continue to model and set healthy boundaries so that the growing adolescent can maintain a healthy sense of self, as the adolescent struggles for self-identity. When the parents are too rigid or too loose in their boundaries and limits, the adolescent will not learn healthy boundaries and will not develop as healthy a sense of self.

It is also during this time that the person usually makes more serious attempts at having an intimate relationship. While these attempts may come and go into and throughout much of adulthood, we can view these relationships as a sort of "practice," even when they are not fulfilling. Until I develop a healthy sense of my True Self, which is built and maintained by my having healthy boundaries, I will likely not be able to have a healthy and fulfilling intimate relationship.

Adolescents in a healthy family get a chance to repeat the first 14 to 16 tasks of child development, as shown in Table 4.1.

Adulthood

As a young adult who is still in the first half of life, it may be difficult to form as healthy a sense of self with healthy boundaries — for a number of reasons. These reasons may include that I am here focused more on getting established as an independent person, apart from my family, which includes a career and perhaps eventually a family of my own. But if I grew up in an unhealthy family, where I did not get the healthy parenting that I needed, probably the most important reason is because I was never taught, modeled and allowed by my family and society to have a healthy self with healthy boundaries. The more unhealthy my family of origin, extended family, and society may be, the more important is this reason. Both healthy and wounded adults continue to cycle through these developmental stages throughout their life.

Development in an Unhealthy Family

Infancy and Early Childhood

In a family where the parents or other parent figures are not themselves self-actualized or recovered, the infant will usually be wounded in an approximate proportion to the extent that the parents are wounded. In such an unhealthy family — with boundary distortions the rule — the parents tend to project their unfinished business onto each other and onto their vulnerable children.[72,78,109]

As in a healthy family, the infant believes that it is a part of and is fused with its parents. And as it gets older, it perceives that it is an extension of its parents. During this time the infant may get either little or no healthy "mirroring" from its parents, or it may get distorted mirroring.

Thus, narcissistic or otherwise distracted parents mistreat and mold the infant to be an extension of their wants and needs (Table 4.1). Part of this abuse, which has also been called "soul murder," can be understood by describing it as being actual projective identification, which I discuss in Chapter 6. Still later, around one year of age, wounded themselves, the parents disallow their child to separate and explore for itself. Unhealthy boundaries are finally solidified by the parents' modeling and demanding that the child-parent boundaries be rigid and/or too loose.

By two years old the child is already being molded into a *distortion* of its potential to learn about its otherwise healthy "sameness" with others into co-dependence, and its otherwise healthy "differentness" into toxic shame and low self-esteem. And in what follows, its boundaries continue to be invaded and distorted, as parents, parent figures and others continue to stifle the child's healthy exploring, creativity and self-esteem.

Latency Age

During latency age, as the child is forced into roles to the detriment of itself, it attempts to separate from its abusers in its own way. This may cover a range that includes over-cooperation as the "good child" to the opposite extreme of being a "delinquent."

Adolescence and Adulthood

In adolescence all of the above may be exaggerated, as the adolescent tries to individuate and separate from unhealthy parents. Because they have had little healthy mirroring or modeling, their attempts to separate may include some destructive or risk-taking behavior, which has often been labeled "acting out." All adolescents "act out" or test the limits in order to learn which boundaries are flexible and which are not. It is when those boundaries are always changing or never bending that an adolescent may "act out" more and more, developing into an unhealthy pattern. These patterns may involve harming others and/or property, and they inevitably cause continuous damage to themselves.

Other adolescents may "act in" to a greater degree than "out," harming mostly themselves, while concerning or even manipulating others. Either way, they are now labeled "the problem child" and the problem or dysfunction in the family, and they can now carry much of the family's emotional weight.

While some people awaken to some or even many of these facts as young adults, most of those who do awaken tend to do so at mid-life or after. From the end of adolescence and throughout our adult life we recycle through our prior developmental tasks and the developmental milestones of healthy boundaries. And after mid-life, if we have not already experienced such, we usually embark on a more conscious search for self and God. It is here that we can begin to learn to let go of some of our rigid boundaries. But before we can let go of anything, we have to know just what it is that we are letting go of. So in recovery we continue our search. And if we persist with safe and supportive people, we ultimately experientially find our Real Self and the God of our understanding.

The Zipper Model of Boundaries

All of the above can result in the person's inability to be fully aware of their inner life and of setting their own boundaries. What happens is that others end up invading both their boundaries and inner life, as though the person had little or no awareness or control of these vital life functions. It may feel as if someone else — from outside of us — is setting our boundaries for us, like a zipper that can be opened and closed from the outside only (Figure 4.1). In recovery, as we heal our True Self, we reclaim these functions by setting our own boundaries, like opening and closing a zipper from the inside.[33]

Paine and Hunt say, "When one has a clear sense of boundaries between the inside and the outside, one is able to develop healthy self-esteem based on a sense of autonomy. Unfortunately parents in alcoholic and unhealthy homes do not have a clear sense of where they end and where their children begin, and they are more interested in controlling their children than in respecting their individuality. Closed doors and the privacy of mail and diaries might be ignored as parents barge into any realm of their children's lives they wish to invade. They may keep their children up into the night sharing adult confidences, and often accuse them of behaviors that are simply projections of the parental turmoil. As a result, these children either don't have a sense that it is okay to say no to people infringing on them, or they become so rigid in their need to defend themselves that they are unable to let anything in.

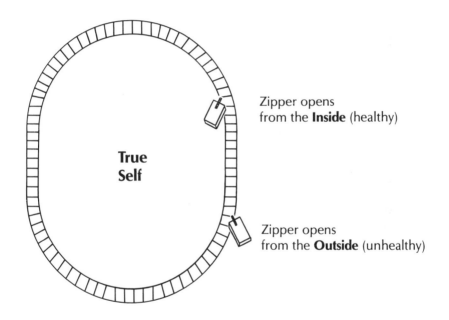

Figure 4.1. The Zipper Model of Boundaries from the Inside (Healthy) and from the Outside (Unhealthy).
(Modified from Fossum and Mason)

"As ACoAs both of us felt at times so pushed and pulled by contradictory parental needs and rules while we were

growing up that by the time we were supposed to act auton-
omously, our personal boundaries were too ill-defined to
function well. We were therefore always dependent on what
other people thought of us, and our lives were roller-coaster
rides of ego boosts and personal attacks."[86]

During this unhealthy developmental sequence, the True
Self thus gets wounded. While this wounding happens differently in type and intensity for each person, it also has
similarities, which I have described in *Co-dependence* and will
now summarize below.[112]

How the True Self Gets Wounded

Like most psychological wounding, this process is largely
unconscious. The following summary of it is taken from several sources, including object relations and self psychology.

1. Wounded themselves, including having unhealthy boundaries, the child's parents feel inadequate, bad, and unfulfilled.

2. They project those charged feelings onto others, especially onto their spouse and their vulnerable children. They
may also project grandiosity (e.g., "I always know what's
best for you!" — when they don't). They look outside themselves to feel whole.

3. In a need to stabilize the parents and to survive, the
child denies that the parents are inadequate and bad. With
the unhealthy boundaries that it has learned from its parents and others, the child internalizes (takes in, introjects,
accepts) the parents' projected inadequacy and badness. A
common fantasy is that, "If I'm really good and perfect, they
will love me and they won't reject or abandon me." The child
idealizes the parents.

4. Because of the above, the child's vulnerable True Self
(in object relations terms: lost heart of the self, libidinal
ego) is wounded so often, that to protect its True Self it
defensively submerges ("splits off") itself deep within the
unconscious part of its psyche. *The Child Goes Into Hiding*
(Figure 4.2).

The Child in hiding represents what may appear at first to be the safest of boundaries, in that it helps us survive. Its down side is that going into hiding and staying there keeps us alienated from the power of knowing and being our True Self.

Figure 4.2. The Child Goes into Hiding

5. The child takes in whatever else it is told — both verbally and nonverbally — about others, and stores it in its unconscious (mostly) and its conscious mind (sometimes and to some degree).

6. What it takes in are messages from major and impactful relationships. The mental representations of these relationships are called "objects" by the object relations theorists. These representations are laden with feelings, and tend to occur in "part-objects" (e.g., good parent, bad parent, aggressive child, shy child and so on).

7. The more self-destructive messages are deposited most often in the false self. This has also been called by object relations theorists the internal saboteur, anti-libidinal ego, or the internalized or introjected, rejecting or otherwise mistreating parent.[122]

8. A tension builds. The True Self is always striving to come alive and to evolve. At the same time, the negative ego (the destructive part of the false self[57b]) attacks the True Self, thus forcing it to stay submerged, keeping self-esteem low. Also the child's grieving of its losses and traumas is not supported. Because of all of the above, the child's development is disordered and its boundaries become unhealthy. This resulting "psychopathology" or "lesion" has been called a schizoid compromise (Guntrip), multiplicity of repressed egos (Fairbairn), and a splitting off of the true self (Winnicott).[122] The outcome can be a developmental delay, arrest or failure.

9. Some results include chronic emptiness, fear, sadness and confusion, and often periodic explosions of self-destructive and other destructive behavior — both impulsive and compulsive — that allows some release of the tension and a glimpse of the True Self.

10. The consequences of the continued emptiness and/or repeated destructive behavior keep the True Self stifled or submerged. The person maintains a low self-esteem, remains unhappy, yet wishes and seeks fulfillment. Compulsions and addictions ("repetition compulsions") can provide temporary fulfillment, but lead to more suffering and ultimately block fulfillment and serenity.

What results from the above described wounding process is co-dependence in its primary form. It can also be called the adult child syndrome or condition. Co-dependence is a practical and expansive concept and state of being that describes some of the most important manifestations of being an adult child of a troubled, unhealthy, or dysfunctional family. I find it most useful to view co-dependence as being a major manifestation of the adult child syndrome.[112]

11. Recovery and growth is discovering and gently unearthing the True Self (Child Within) so that it can exist and express itself in a healthy way, day to day (Figure 4.2). They also include restructuring the false self or ego to become a more flexible assistant (positive ego) to the True Self.[57b] Some other results: aliveness, creativity and growth.

12. Such self-discovery and recovery is most effectively accomplished gradually and in the presence of safe, compassionate, skilled and supportive people. With commitment to and active participation in recovery, this healing process may take from three to five years or more.[112]

Recovery and Development

In recovery we get a second chance to retrace and complete the developmental tasks that we never got to finish before. But that chance is not given *to* us, because in recovery we can learn that no one else any longer determines our destiny. Rather, by our own motivation and by setting healthy boundaries, *we create it.* By choosing recovery and risking to be real, we set the healthy boundaries that say, "I am in charge of my recovery and my life, and no one else on this Earth is."

Part of that claiming of our personal power may include, if we choose, our *letting go* of our prior perhaps rigid and therefore unhealthy boundaries or walls, and letting selected safe and supportive others *in* to assist us in our recovery. These may include any one or more of a number of people in our life, such as a best friend, therapist, therapy group, self-help group, sponsor or any other safe and supportive person that we might choose. And it may also include our Higher Power.

Setting and maintaining healthy boundaries thus protects the integrity and well-being of the True Self in a healthy cycle, since it is the *True Self* that by its own internal resources *sets the boundary,* which then allows it to stay out of hiding, as shown in Figure 4.3.

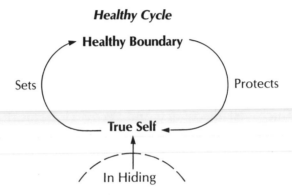

Healthy Cycle

Figure 4.3. The Protective and Nourishing Cycle of Self-Generated Boundaries, which allow the True Self (Child Within) to come out of hiding and eventually stay out

This process of recovery is not easy. It takes patience and persistence, a dedication to healing my True Self, my Child Within, over a long duration of time. While learning to set healthy boundaries and limits is crucial in this process, so is learning both cognitively and experientially about the phenomenon of age regression, which I next address.

5

Boundaries And Age Regression

Just learning about age regression can be healing. An important reason for this is because it is a major teacher about both unhealthy and healthy boundaries.

Age regression happens when we suddenly feel upset, confused and scared, like a helpless little child. There may be no apparent cause for it, and it may last a few minutes or longer. It can feel as though one minute we are an adult, feeling okay, and in a matter of seconds we feel like an out-of-control and helpless little person. Has anything like that ever happened to you?

We can begin to heal ourselves around such an age regression when one happens by beginning to observe our inner life and what is happening around us. (See Figure 1.3.) As we heal our Child Within, we can discover that while it is painful and debilitating, age regression is actually a healing gift in disguise. For one thing, it can teach us about boundaries. This is because the genesis of age regression and its recurrence throughout childhood, adolescence and adulthood nearly always means the same thing. Our boundaries

61

are being invaded, they are about to be invaded, or this particular experience that I am having right this minute is somehow reminding me of a past experience when my boundaries were invaded.

Age regression can arise in many and various circumstances, such as when someone yells at us or shames us in some way. These may include a comment about our weight or a mistake we may have made. There is therefore usually a *trigger* that initiates the rapid sequence of age regression. This trigger may be any of number of possibilities, including any mistreatment or abandonment by anyone, any negative message from anyone, any form of invalidation or anything that reminds us of any of the above.

We can age regress at any time, in any place and for any reason. Immediately after the triggering event, we may suddenly feel the following in *rapid sequence:* fear, hurt, shame, guilt, anger, confusion and disorientation. We may end up feeling dysfunctional and out of control, almost as if we want to scream. But our True Self feels too weak even for that, so it may want just to go back into hiding.

When age regression continues to wound us repeatedly, with no healing around it, we may remain paralyzed, confused and dysfunctional, and our True Self stays in hiding. When we recognize it and heal it, age regression can be a useful opportunity in our healing and well-being. To heal it we recognize it, work through it and learn from it. To do all of this can take many months and more often several years in a full recovery program. [112,116]

Healing Age Regression

The first step in healing age regression is to *recognize* it when it happens. This is a kind of self-diagnosis. Visiting our family of origin is often an opportune time to self-diagnose age regression because we tend to get mistreated, mentally or emotionally abandoned or invalidated there so frequently. When it happens, I might say to myself something like, "Hey, I'm age regressing now," or "I just age regressed." This is a great moment, because when we name it, we can do something about it.

We can then begin to take some slow deep breaths. And then begin to walk around the room. (The point is not to be immobilized, since that may contribute to perpetuating our feeling of immobilization and helplessness.) Then begin to look at various objects in the room. Walk into another room and do the same.

We can also pick up our keys and begin to play with them. Keys are symbolic of freedom. They open doors and start car engines. An accompanying practice in preventing and managing the sometimes crippling effects of age regression is, when convenient, to always *have a way out* of our family member's house or any other potentially toxic environment if the going gets too difficult. We can bring our car with us, stay in a motel or have some other way to get out should we need to. Doing so is a way of setting healthy boundaries so that our True Self can begin to process it all.

Processing the Experience

As soon as possible, talk about it with a safe person. This is why, when convenient, it can be helpful to bring a safe person with us when we visit — *or* when an unsafe person visits us. If there is no one to talk with, perhaps we can call a friend or write down what happened and how it felt, and then talk it over with a safe person later. Even later we can talk about it some more. This is a great healing opportunity, and it can be most helpful to talk it over with our therapy group, therapist or other safe person or people.

It is helpful eventually to work through what happened and how it felt during the age regression in a deeper and experiential way. Some techniques to facilitate this include telling our story, anger bat work, writing and reading (to a safe person) an unmailed letter, family sculpture, gestalt techniques and any creative technique.[116]

Then consider the *levels of meaning* that the age regression may have for us. For example:

Level 1 — I was mistreated in the past.
    2 — I am being mistreated now.
    3 — I don't want to be mistreated anymore.
    4 — I'm going to set firm boundaries and limits in this relationship.
    5 — I'm going to take a break from or possibly even leave this relationship if the mistreatment continues.
    6 — I can get free of this unnecessary pain and suffering.
    7 — I am learning and growing from my awareness of this age regression.
    8 — By using it, I am healing my True Self.

At about Level 5 above, people sometimes may feel as if they are being mistreated without looking at their role in the mistreatment. Or perhaps they may be also mistreating their partner, such as intruding on their partner's boundaries without realizing it. They may not realize how their words or behavior may be invading their partner's boundaries in a sometimes subtle way.

We recognize these triggers and other triggering events as they come up for us. By doing so, we can then avoid situations where we may anticipate they will happen. Finally, we can use all of the above constructively. We can begin to recognize and heal any future age regressions, avoid or minimize contact with people who do triggering behaviors, protect our Child Within, stop blaming ourself, and bring the unconscious in our life more into our full awareness.

Further Meanings

When approached in a conscious, self-caring way, age regressions can be healing since they get us in touch with our past unhealed injuries. We heal ourselves in this way in a safe environment. If we are continually exposed to mistreatment, we can heal an age regression in a safe place such as our therapy group, a similar support group or individual counseling. For some people, age regressions may be associated with panic attacks, and the above steps can be helpful in handling some panic attacks.

Age regression is a sudden decompensation that is triggered by a hurt that is nearly always due to an actual or a possible boundary invasion. It occurs commonly among adult children of unhealthy families and in people with post-traumatic stress disorder (PTSD).

Three Kinds of Age Regression

In recovery we discover that there are three kinds of age regression. The first is as described above, wherein we end up with a paralyzed or passive state and feeling. The second may have the same triggers and feelings, but we become much more active. For example, we may throw a temper tantrum, at times even verbally attacking someone close to us. Or we may express pain by crying and even some shaking or contorting of our body.

The third type is a "therapeutic" variety of age regression, wherein either or a combination of the above two types occurs during the normal and constructive course of group or individual therapy. In this latter type in a safe and supportive environment, we can heal more easily, although if we are with safe others outside of a therapeutic context we can also heal to some extent.

All three of these kinds of age regression generate conflict. We can use the occurrence of both the age regression and the conflict to help us go deeper into our pain and to heal. This intense feeling of conflict is a part of the phenomenon and defense known as *transference* or *projection*. It can be experienced on at least three levels:

1. With those people with whom I am in *current* conflict.
2. With what the current experience *reminds* me of. (This is a deeper level that addresses past unfinished hurts.)
3. With what *old tapes* or messages I may be playing in my own mind about all of this. (This is the deepest level, and the way that I may often beat myself up.)

To heal age regression, we need to have safe, close people to assist us. Learning about age regression opens doors to the richness and opportunity that lie deep within our inner life, and it helps us begin to sort out each of our feelings.

Conclusion

Boundary invasions by one or more members of our family of origin, as well as by others, are usually the initial cause of age regression. And boundary invasions, or the suggestion of them, may be the trigger for subsequent age regressions throughout our life — until we get into recovery and learn about them both cognitively and experientially.

While age regression may be either dramatic or subtle, another form of boundary distortion that is usually subtle, though common, is projective identification, which I address in the next chapter.

6

Giving And Receiving: Boundaries And Projective Identification

Giving and receiving are core dynamics in relationships, whether they ·are healthy or unhealthy. Learning about *projective identification* as an unhealthy dynamic can open us to understanding the nature of healthy interactions, which can lead to a richer and satisfying experience of intimacy. This experience can also help us learn even more about our boundaries, which can be empowering in our recovery.

Over the years, psychologists and other therapists have given the phenomenon of projective identification many names, including: trading of dissociations, irrational role assignment, scapegoating, identifying with the aggressor, evocation of a proxy, split-off part objects, joint personality, family projection process, fusion, enmeshment and family ego mass.[85,125] These are all about the same general process, which occurs frequently in unrecovered adult children of unhealthy families.[112]

Definitions and Genesis

While many writers have attempted to define this complex process of projective identification, it is difficult to come up with a simple yet comprehensive definition.* One of the clearest is by Cashdan, who defines projective identifications as: "patterns of interpersonal behavior in which a person induces others to behave or respond in a circumscribed fashion. This differs from ordinary projection, which is essentially a mental act and need not involve overt responses of any sort."[20]

My briefest definition is that in projective identification, one person denies or disowns a part of their own inner life and induces another to take on and act out that disowned part, while frequently blaming the receiver for doing so. Before recovery, which includes the formation of healthy boundaries, the entire process is unconscious to both partners of the relationship. It is often not even noticed by unaware observers.

Projective identification is one of the most complex yet subtle of all the ways we have to defend against experiencing and handling emotional pain. It is also one of the most destructive and dysfunctional. It comes about from a combination of both healthy and unhealthy developmental mechanisms, which begin in early infancy.

Perhaps our two earliest defenses against emotional pain** are splitting (all-or-none thinking and behaving) and projection. Wanting to relate, grow and develop, the infant uses its parents and others in its outer life to get to know and experience its inner life. The infant and child use others

---

*For example, expanding on Klein's descriptions in the 1930s, Segal defines projective identification as being "the result of the projection of parts of the self into an object. It may result in the object's being perceived as having acquired the characteristics of the projected parts of the self, but it can also result in the self becoming identified with the object of its projection."[55,68,97] Although this observation was somewhat helpful to psychologists in the 1960s, it can also show how this kind of jargon can confuse and distance us from the reality of our actual inner life experience.

** Based on current understandings of psychological mechanisms, e.g., from object relations, and self psychology and others, where we have come to differentiate the True Self from the ego, I view the terms "ego defenses" and "ego dynamics" to be confusing and inaccurate. Here I prefer to use *defenses against pain* (i.e., emotional pain) over "ego defenses."

as models, mirrors and relationships. If these are unhealthy, the infant and child get a distorted view of themselves and of others.

Ideally, as it grows, the child learns to sort out all-or-none thinking and projection in a healthy way to progressively more sophisticated levels. Eventually it can see and choose among the gray expanse between the "all" and the "none," as well as become able to own its own inner life rather than disown and project it. However, in an unhealthy family and society, what develops for the child is a number of unhealthy ways of handling pain, one of which is projective identification. As described in Chapter 4, during this phase of unhealthy growth and development the infant and child also learn unhealthy boundaries. These interdigitate and interact with the formation of projective identification as a defense against emotional pain. As we heal in recovery, we can learn much about healthy and unhealthy boundaries by cognitively and experientially learning about projective identification.

Projective identification has been described as occurring in as few as three and as many as eight stages.[85,99] I find it easiest to understand when arranged in a sequence of five stages or events, as shown in Figure 6.1. In each of these stages there may be either healthy or unhealthy aspects of the general process of giving and receiving in a particular relationship.

Five-Part Sequence of Giving and Receiving

Projective identification begins when (1) I unconsciously relate to another person (the "object" in object relations psychology terms) by sharing a part of my inner life ("parts of the self") with them. (Item 1 in Figure 6.1.)

By contrast, in healthy giving and receiving, I consciously share parts of my inner life with another. This sharing may include any feeling, need, wish, expectation or idea that I may want to extend, give, connect or heal (project) to or with you, or about which I may want to be affirmed.[25] Finally,

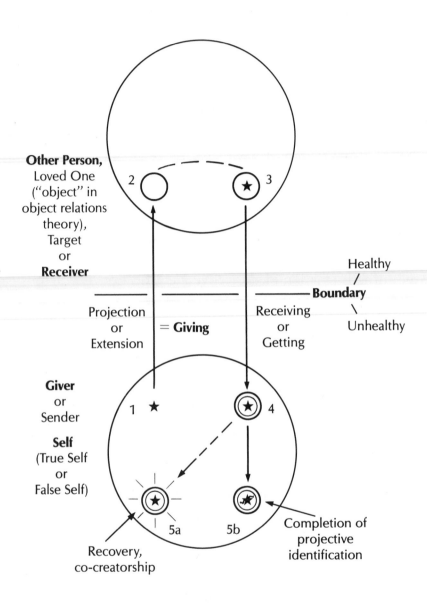

Other Person,
Loved One
("object" in
object relations
theory),
Target
or
Receiver

Healthy
/
━━━━━ **Boundary**
\
Unhealthy

Projection
or
Extension

= **Giving**

Receiving
or
Getting

Giver
or
Sender

Self
(True Self
or
False Self)

Completion of
projective
identification

Recovery,
co-creatorship

**Figure 6.1. Cycle of Giving and Receiving
in Human Interaction**

like this step and all of the following ones, this inner life material may be either that which I have *made* or *received* from another person, or both.

Whatever message I send to you may be mostly about me. Or it may be about aspects of each of us. But (2) what you do with that message will be related to your inner life and your ability to respond (Figure 6.1). And so, based on those factors, (3) you may respond by sending me a message in return. This return communication may be your extension or projection of whatever you think, perceive and experience about what I originally sent to you. Next in the sequence is (4) my perception of what you sent to me, which is what I take in or experience from you in return.

Each of these steps generates thoughts, feelings and other bits of inner life experience in both of us. What we do with all of this depends on the perspective from which we are experiencing our life in the moment. If I am living as my True Self (Item 5a), for example, then I may use my experience to grow as a co-creator of my life.* If all of the above interchange is healthy, I may feel affirmed and have a more accurate and expanded sense of myself. And when there is conflict and pain, I may grow from the experience.

But all of the above (in items 1-5a) is still not projective identification, because I have remained with full awareness as my True Self and with healthy boundaries. I have not taken on anything that is not actually mine or tried to give you anything that is not yours. Rather than being projective identification, it is instead a *healthy interaction*.

---

* *Co-creation* is when I manage my own life as my authentic self in concert with the God of my understanding. I describe it in the last chapter of *Co-dependence — Healing the Human Condition*.

Examples of Projective Identification

However, if I ignore my True Self and identify with and exist from my false or co-dependent self, then I may stagnate or regress and remain feeling like a martyr/victim, with a contracted sense of myself. I unconsciously project onto you a part of my inner life that I want you to take on for me. This projective identification may also allow me to continue to deny or disown that part of my inner life that I may have tried to project onto you. For example, if I am angry or resentful about something and I don't want to feel and handle that feeling, then I can unconsciously dump (project) it onto you. If you buy it, also unconsciously, and act it out by expressing it for me to others and also back to me, then I won't have to own and deal with my own feelings of anger and resentment. What is more, if you express your now taken-on anger "too much" to others and to me, I will criticize and berate you — or hold it against you in some other way — for being so angry so often.[98]

Or if I feel ashamed and inadequate, and I don't want to feel and handle that feeling of shame, then I can likewise unconsciously attempt to transfer my feeling to you. And if you unconsciously buy it, then you can *act it out* and perhaps even *express* it for me. Then I can shame you even more for being so inadequate (Table 6.1 on page 74-76).

Notice that in these examples (Table 6.1), nearly every message and movement is delivered and proceeds *unconsciously*, just as do nearly all of the same dynamics in unrecovered co-dependence. In fact, this dynamic is an example of co-dependence in action. This is in contrast to healthy interaction, where the giving and receiving tend to occur on a more conscious level of awareness on the parts of both people.

To use projective identification requires the unhealthy co-operation, also unconscious, of two or more people. Both partners are here actively co-dependent because each has a lost self. Each is focusing (that is, projecting, using and blaming) on the other, their partner, to their own detriment. They are also each operating with unhealthy boundaries which allow this destructive dynamic to complete its vicious cycle.

We learned this detrimental defense the same place that we learned most of our other defenses against emotional pain: from our dysfunctional relationships. In our family of origin and elsewhere we watched others model it, and we found that it may have helped us to survive the overwhelming pain of all those unhealthy relationships. Fortunately, what is learned can also be unlearned.

Healing Projective Identifications

To heal our attachment to this damaging and eventually imprisoning defense is to heal our True Self. Three basic and interrelated actions and processes that are especially important here include:

1. Realizing our True Self
2. Bringing the unconscious material of our inner life into our conscious awareness and owning it
3. Setting healthy boundaries and limits.

Boundaries are key here, as shown in Figure 6.1. If we have unhealthy boundaries, we are like sponges that absorb the painful conflicted material others send from their inner life. It is clearly not ours, yet we soak it up. Unless we have healthy boundaries, others may absorb whatever of ours that we send back to them. To have a healthy relationship, we each need healthy boundaries.

Table 6.1. Giving and Receiving: Projective Identification in Co-dependence, with Some Dynamics and Examples

Description of Dynamics	Individual Dynamics Examples B. Co-dependent Cycle with Anger
A. Healthy Interaction	
1. Aspect of my inner life needing connection, sharing, affirmation, extension or healing (projection). For example: a feeling, need, wish, expectation or idea. This material is received from another or made by me.	Unconsciously angry and resentful of parental abuse as a child, Dick projects his anger onto Jane. He does not fully experience or own his anger, but unconsciously entices her to feel and express his anger for him.
2. Other's material and ability to respond. Received or made.	Jane has some unhealed anger of her own and unconsciously takes on Dick's projected anger.
3. Other's response, extension or projection. Received or made.	Jane openly expresses this anger at Dick's parents, at others and back to Dick.
4. My perception. What I take in or experience. Received *and* made.	Relieved of the responsibility of handling his own anger, Dick perceives Jane as being too angry and resentful, and criticizes her for it. He remains calm and in control.
5a. Staying fully aware in my True Self, I use my experience to grow as a co-creator. Affirmation. Expanded sense of self. Co-created. Healthy interaction.	Potential space for transformation and healing.
5b. Ignoring my True Self, coming mostly from my false self, I stagnate or regress and remain as a martyr/victim. Contracted sense of self. Continue to disown part of me. Made. *Projective identification.*	Unaware of his True Self, Dick lives from his false self, remaining Jane's martyr/victim (as she is his). This allows him to continue to disown his still unexpressed anger, which continues to build and make him ill. They both avoid intimacy and blame the other for their unfulfillment.

C. Co-dependent Cycle with Shame

★ 1. Roy is unconsciously ashamed and feeling inadequate from being abused as a child. He projects his shame and inadequacy onto his employee, Jim. Instead of helping or supporting him, Roy shames and berates Jim for any slight mistakes.

○ 2. Jim has unhealed shame from his own family of origin, and unconsciously takes on Roy's projected shame.

⊛ 3. Hoping for Roy's and other's support, Jim openly talks of his mistakes when they occur, while protecting Roy from taking responsibility for Roy's own mistakes.

◎ 4. Roy continues to shame and berate Jim, including what he terms Jim's "lack of enthusiasm and involvement" in assisting Roy with their business.

⊛ 5a. Potential space for transformation and healing.

◉ 5b. Unaware of his True Self, Roy lives from his false self, and criticizes Jim even more for being a "wimp" and a victim. This allows Roy to continue to disown his own shame, which continues to make him ill. They both avoid working together constructively, and blame the other for their pain.

D. Co-dependence Transformed to Healthy Boundaries

Peg, an elderly parent, projects to her adult child Kim the responsibility for helping Peg with her conflicts and pain.

Hero and caretaker, Kim wants to help and perhaps even fix her mother, and begins listening. Staying awake to her inner life, she soon becomes uncomfortable and realizes that this exchange is inappropriate.

Kim tells her mother politely that she is uncomfortable in this role, thus visualizing and strengthening her boundaries. Kim suggests that Peg needs her own therapist.

At first Peg responds by being confused and hurt. A few days later, however, Peg finds peers and a therapist with whom to talk.

Peg uses these new supports to begin to realize her True Self and to begin to learn her own healthy boundaries. Kim and Peg each begin to learn to extend uncondi-tional love to the other. At times Peg reverts back to asking her daughter for help with her conflicts and pain. When this happens, both recognize it and re-establish healthy boundaries.

E. Cycles of Extending Unconditional Love

1. Even though they have conflicts which they continue to work through, Marshall extends love to Barbara.

2. Previously uncertain of Marshall's love, Barbara now recognizes that love. She affirms and receives it.

3. Barbara then returns her love to Marshall.

4. Marshall openly receives Barbara's love and feels expanded by it.

5a. Marshall extends more love back to Barbara progressively and unconditionally. Both begin to experience their relationship as safe and trusting.

5b. At times Marshall reverts back to withholding love from her, and he begins to feel progressively increasing pain. Eventually, he remembers the love, often asking his Higher Power for assistance, and re-extends his unconditional love to Barbara. Their relationship continues to grow.

READER/CUSTOMER CARE SURVEY

HEFG

We care about your opinions! Please take a moment to fill out our online Reader Survey at **http://survey.hcibooks.com.**
As a **"THANK YOU"** you will receive a **VALUABLE INSTANT COUPON** towards future book purchases as well as a **SPECIAL GIFT** available only online! Or, you may mail this card back to us and we will send you a copy of our exciting catalog with your valuable coupon inside.
(PLEASE PRINT IN ALL CAPS)

First Name _____ MI. _____ Last Name _____

Address _____

State _____ Zip _____ Email _____ City _____

1. Gender
☐ Female ☐ Male

2. Age
☐ 8 or younger
☐ 9-12   ☐ 13-16
☐ 17-20   ☐ 21-30
☐ 31+

3. Did you receive this book as a gift?
☐ Yes   ☐ No

4. Annual Household Income
☐ under $25,000
☐ $25,000 - $34,999
☐ $35,000 - $49,999
☐ $50,000 - $74,999
☐ over $75,000

5. What are the ages of the children living in your house?
☐ 0 - 14   ☐ 15+

6. Marital Status
☐ Single
☐ Married
☐ Divorced
☐ Widowed

7. How did you find out about the book?
(please choose one)
☐ Recommendation
☐ Store Display
☐ Online
☐ Catalog/Mailing
☐ Interview/Review

8. Where do you usually buy books?
(please choose one)
☐ Bookstore
☐ Online
☐ Book Club/Mail Order
☐ Price Club (Sam's Club, Costco's, etc.)
☐ Retail Store (Target, Wal-Mart, etc.)

9. What subject do you enjoy reading about the most?
(please choose one)
☐ Parenting/Family
☐ Relationships
☐ Recovery/Addictions
☐ Health/Nutrition
☐ Christianity
☐ Spirituality/Inspiration
☐ Business Self-help
☐ Women's Issues
☐ Sports

10. What attracts you most to a book?
(please choose one)
☐ Title
☐ Cover Design
☐ Author
☐ Content

TAPE IN MIDDLE; DO NOT STAPLE

FOLD HERE

Comments

We can begin to bring our unconscious material, which is related to our unfinished business, up into our conscious awareness in countless ways — ways that we can learn during the long course of the recovery process. While there are several examples of bringing unconscious material in projective identification into our conscious awareness as part of the healing process, the following is an example wherein several dynamics, including P.I., were operative.

> **Joe** was a 40-year-old man who grew up with an over-controlling mother who told him and other family members what to feel and what to do, and she still does. Although this was frustrating and hurtful for him even as an adult, he still waits for others to tell him what to do. This causes him to have serious problems in most of his relationships.
>
> Robbed of his inner life, he didn't know his Real Self. His mother repeatedly invaded his boundaries as she attacked the integrity and well-being of his True Self. But until his recovery, most of these dynamics were unconscious to him — they were outside of his awareness.
>
> Early in his recovery he felt guilty for telling the truth of his experience, which he sometimes interpreted as saying bad things about his parents. Later, he felt helpless over not being able to change the way his mother treated him. He began to see that the only thing he could change was the way he reacted to her. The only thing he could change was himself. In his therapy group and in individual therapy he learned to grieve the pain of these ungrieved traumas and to begin to set healthier boundaries and limits with his parents and others.

Once we begin to bring any of our unconscious material into our conscious awareness — whether related to projective identification or not — it will become progressively easier to recognize and heal our unconscious hurts, traumas and repetition compulsions. It will also be easier for us to prevent stuffing (repressing and suppressing) present ones. In fact, rather than stuff them, we will experience them and use them for our growth and well-being.

While projective identification is mostly destructive to individuals and their relationships, it also has a few things to offer in recovery. Ogden has described four levels of usefulness of the process of projective identification.[85] The first three are the most primitive, wherein the process may be used as a defense, an attempted communication and a transitional experience (Table 6.2). The fourth and most empowering level is using projective identification as an opportunity for growth. We can discover this over the long process of our recovery.

Table 6.2. Levels of Usefulness of the Process in Projective Identification (compiled and modified from Ogden 1991)

Defense — serves to create a sense of psychological distance from my painful and unwanted experiences and other parts of my inner life.

Communication — I induce in you feelings and experiences similar to my own so that you can understand me better and we can feel as if we are more together.

Transitional experience — by giving my unwanted experience to you, without owning it myself, I can explore it from a distance.

Growth opportunity — sensing my experience in you, and working through our associated conflict, I now own my own experience and heal some of my unfinished business.

Conclusion

Being aware of and expressing parts of our inner life without dumping them onto others is a delicate balance. Hearing the shared inner life of others without taking on — and in — what is not ours is also empowering. Healthy boundaries help us in this balance. Table 6.1 shows examples of these dynamics in healthy interactions in columns D and E.

We get what we give. If we give out pain (projection), we get more pain in return. If we give (extend) love, we get more love in return. Understanding these principles and dynamics can help us heal our woundedness.[25]

In Table 6.3 I summarize some components of healthy and unhealthy interactions. In a healthy interaction, I am living mostly from my True Self with a conscious awareness of much of my inner life, and I have healthy boundaries. And as my partner in this healthy interaction, you will ideally do the same.

In an unhealthy interaction, whether or not there may be projective identification, both people will tend to operate from their false self. They will have little awareness of or responsibility for their inner life, and they will have unhealthy boundaries.

Table 6.3. Some Characteristics of Healthy and Unhealthy Interactions in Relationships

Type of Interaction	Healthy	Unhealthy
I Live from my	True Self	False self
Awareness	Conscious	Unconscious
Take Responsibility for my Inner Life	Yes	No
Healthy Boundaries		

But it is not always easy to sort out what is from my inner life and what is from yours. I describe some principles that may be useful in addressing these in the next two chapters.

7

What Is Mine?
What Is Not Mine?
Sorting And Owning – *Part One*

Learning about the defense of projective identification can help me begin to sort out psychologically what is mine and what is yours. But just *knowing* about it doesn't mean that what either one of us proclaims belongs to the other is actually so. In fact, such indiscriminate proclamations can themselves constitute boundary invasions.

It is a delicate balance. It takes vigilance and practice, often with lots of trial and error, before I can become more comfortable in sorting and owning what is mine and knowing what is not mine.

What Is Mine?

To help sort out what is mine in a relationship, probably the most important action I can take is to *pay attention to my inner life* (Figure 1.1, page 2). My inner life contains such things as my beliefs, thoughts, feelings, decisions, choices, experiences, wants, needs, sensations and intuitions. It also

includes unconscious experiences such as dreams and fantasies, repetition compulsions and other unfinished business.
The more I get to know my True Self and its inner life
clearly, the more I will likely know what is actually mine in
any relationship.

Going Deeper — Using Experiential Aids

The problem comes when I cannot yet recognize some of
my inner life experiences and material that are *unconscious*
— not yet in my conscious awareness. One approach to
bringing my unconscious material into my conscious awareness is to use any of a number of experiential techniques,
such as risking and sharing, telling my story, working
through transference and dream analysis. Using these experiential techniques can open the gates of the unconscious,
so I can begin to experience what I may have stored there.
I describe 21 experiential aids that can assist in the process
of recovery and in everyday life in *A Gift to Myself*, here
reproduced as Table 7.1.

A way that I can begin to experience my powerful inner
life more is to choose more of these techniques that may
help to facilitate my experiencing. Such experiential healing
techniques tend to have some of the following characteristics in common:

Being Real — We tend to be our Real or True Self
when we are using them, although in the beginning we
may feel uncomfortable.

Focused — We are focused on an aspect of our inner
life.

Structured — There is a structure or form to the
technique itself.

Safe — To be most healing, it is generally done in a
safe and supportive environment.

As feelings and other material come up, I can share them
with one or more appropriate safe people and then work

Table 7.1. Some Experiential Techniques for Healing Our Child Within (True Self)

1. Risking and sharing, especially feelings, with safe and supportive people

2. Storytelling (telling our own story, including risking and sharing)

3. Working through transference (what we project or "transfer" onto others, and vice versa for them)

4. Psychodrama and its variations: Reconstruction, Gestalt Therapy and Family Sculpture

5. Hypnosis and related techniques

6. Attending Self-Help Meetings

7. Working the Twelve Steps (of AA, Al-Anon, CoDA, NA, OA, etc.)

8. Group Therapy (usually a safe and supportive place to practice many of these experiential techniques

9. Couples Therapy or Family Therapy

10. Guided Imagery

11. Breathwork

12. Affirmations

13. Dream Analysis

14. Art, Movement and Play Therapy

15. Active Imagination, using Intuition and Voice Dialogue

16. Meditation and Prayer

17. Therapeutic Bodywork

18. Keeping a journal or a diary

19. Writing an unmailed letter

20. Using a workbook like *A Gift to Myself*

21. Creating our own experiential techniques or healing

These experiential techniques ideally should be used in the context of a full recovery program, as described throughout *A Gift to Myself* and *Co-dependence* through them toward a healthy resolution. I describe this process in more detail in Chapters 17 and 18 on "Experiencing" in *A Gift to Myself*. While all of these may facilitate the grieving process, some of them, such as psychodrama, group therapy and breathwork, may facilitate a more dramatic kind of grieving called *abreaction*, which I describe below.

Strong Reactions

Another way to explore my inner life in more depth is to take notice when I may have a strong emotional reaction to any person, place, or thing. Here the *strength* of my reaction is usually inappropriate for the degree or intensity of the stimulus that may be triggering my reaction right now.

> For example, when I traveled on an airplane and heard the sound of someone repeatedly shuffling a deck of playing cards, I would become agitated and angry, almost as though I would like to run up to the person and strangle them. It took me a while to sort out why I was having this strong reaction. On my next flight I used the experiential technique of a self-guided imagery. In that imagery it came to me that when I was a child and trying to sleep at night, my parents and their friends would shuffle and play cards loudly in the next room, and it was hard for me to sleep. I had stuffed some of my anger from these experiences over all these years, and these present sounds triggered my feelings associated with these memories. I used this experience as one of many aids in my own recovery as an adult child of an unhealthy family. Nowadays when I hear these same noises, I still have that reaction. But it is not nearly as strong, and I immediately remember the association and am able to let go of it.

> Another example was the way **Susan** cringed when she heard the sound of ice cubes falling into an empty glass. Her father was an alcoholic and her mother a dysfunctional enabler of his continued drinking. She used this experience as a trigger to remembering old childhood traumas as one aid in her recovery.

Almost anything, including sounds, sights, smells, touches, words and even situations, such as conflicts, can trigger these strong reactions. These triggers remind us in some way of past, unhealed hurts, losses or traumas.

These kinds of traumatic experiences nearly always contain some sort of boundary invasion that harms our delicate and sensitive True Self. As a reaction to that trauma, the True Self generates energy that can be used to heal itself from the trauma, just as healthy tissue grows into a cut in the skin to heal itself. This energy usually has an associated component of emotional pain. But if the energy and its pain are stifled, repressed or not allowed to be expressed, the True Self will store them both in the unconscious part of itself. All of the above usually saps our vitality, creativity and joy. Over time, if it is not used for healing, that energy and pain will resurface as some sort of patterned expression or *repetition compulsion* in an attempt to heal.

Blocks to the Healing

There are usually two factors that tend to block these repeated attempts at healing our old unhealed hurts, losses or traumas. One is our own *psychological defenses* against the emotional pain of dealing with the stored energy. The other is still more *boundary invasions* by others. These boundary invasions may range across a spectrum of the unhealthy boundary invasions described throughout this book: from subtle invalidations to aggressive attacks by others. We may be repeatedly trying to express ourselves in our attempts to heal, and others won't let us.

These blocking boundary invasions may come from an individual, our family or society. They may be in the form of a range of factors, from beliefs and assumptions that are encoded in our minds and block the True Self's free expression, to outright invasive actions and behaviors. Any of these blocks may be ingrained and supported by the individuals and groups that prevent that free expression.

These groups may include our educational system, religions, helping professions, the media, business, law enforcement and government.

A common example of these latter kinds of blocks is when a person is actively grieving or has stuck grief — ungrieved pain from the past — and a helping professional tells them that they are "depressed" and they need drugs to feel better. The boundary invasions here are pushing a likely inaccurate name to describe their condition and giving them drugs instead of assisting them in their healthy grieving. I discuss these more subtle kinds of boundary invasions further in Chapters 19 and 20 of *Co-dependence — Healing the Human Condition* and in *Feelings*.

These and countless other examples are why we need a safe and supportive environment from which to look within at our inner life, experience what is there, own it, work through it and then let it go. It is during each of these actions that we continue to sort out just what is ours and what is not ours.

Abreactions

Any strong reaction like the above can build in intensity until it develops so much movement of its energy that the emotion and expression pours out of the person in one way or another. This is called an *abreaction,* which is an outpouring of previously unexpressed psychic pain and energy. If the abreacting person has a safe and supportive environment, including people who *accept* their expression of pain and *do not invalidate* them, then they have a chance to heal their associated ungrieved grief.

> **Pat** was a 22-year-old college student who grew up in a troubled family. She had repeatedly experienced much discomfort and fear when she and her boyfriend had tried to be physically and sexually intimate but was never able to understand why. One weekend while visiting her mother, some of these feelings began to surface spontaneously, and

she began to cry. As she walked down the steps to the basement where her mother was working, an associated memory of having been sexually abused by her maternal grandfather came to her. (She had been abused in that basement at age nine, and walking down those same steps while having those feelings helped trigger the memories.) At that instant her terror and grief poured out, as she screamed and cried, telling her mother about it all.

What was so healing for Pat was that not only had she *expressed* her grief and told the truth of her experience, but her mother *believed* and *supported* her. Her mother then helped her find a counselor to see and work further through her pain. Had she not believed and supported her, Pat would likely have been doubly traumatized. And that nonsupport would also have been a *boundary invasion,* in that her mother would have invaded and invalidated Pat's true experience.

This is an example of an abreaction. Through her own abilities and motivation, and with the help of her mother's support and many counseling sessions, Pat was able to sort out, own and work through the pain of that past, ungrieved trauma. By doing so, she was also able to strengthen her boundaries. She pushed away and said no when her uncle made a pass at her a year later.

An abreaction is an extreme and dramatic kind of age regression. When recognized and supported in a safe setting during recovery, such an experience can be an important part of the healing process. In fact, I believe that an abreaction may be a natural continuation and extension of age regression, given a safe environment and *validation* of the person's experience on the continuum of a traumatic experience (Figure 7.1).

When a hurt, loss or trauma happens to us, we have a natural tendency to heal it by the grieving process. Even though as children we already know how to grieve, we have to be supported and to feel safe to express that grief so that we can heal, and then let go of its painful energy. To

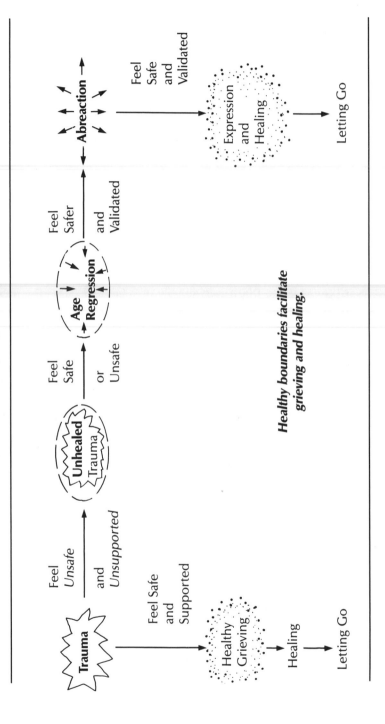

Figure 7.1. The Continuum of a Traumatic Event and Attempting to Heal It

see our parents model their own healthy grief will support and further teach us this process. But if we feel unsupported, with no such healthy modeling, and if we feel unsafe in expressing our pain, we will store that unexpressed energy as an unhealed trauma. One manifestation of the trauma may be repeated age regression, and another and more dramatic manifestation may follow as an abreaction, as we continue attempting to heal the past traumatic experience.

A key to the orderly flow of this healing process is feeling safe, supported and validated by others, which includes the absence of these others invading our boundaries. Support for a child or an adult by healthy parents or others, by skilled therapists or by safe peers, such as in a therapy group, provides a safe and nourishing "holding environment" where the wounded person can express the pain of their grief, and thereby heal.*

Feedback from Safe Others

Feedback from safe others can also help in sorting out what is mine and not mine. But it can be difficult to get honest and appropriate feedback, since many people may be either reluctant or unable to give it. The most helpful, constructive and healing feedback may include any of the following:

What I *see*	How I can *identify* with you
What I *hear*	What came up for me in *my inner life* when I heard your story.

Advice and suggestions are usually not as helpful. Defensiveness, judgment or attacks are often destructive to the relationship.[116]

Feedback is different from sharing in ordinary conversation, wherein a person shares material from *their* inner life,

---

* The Appendix continues a discussion by author and massage therapist Barbara Harris of boundaries and energy from a physical, emotional and spiritual perspective.

such as their experiences, wants, needs, observations and opinions. I discuss feedback further below, under "Getting Help from Safe Others."

The Complexity of Learning from Feedback and Repetition Compulsions

It is not always easy to listen to others' feedback or to become aware of our repetition compulsions (when we make the same mistakes over and over). To do so takes the courage to work through a long-term program of recovery, usually over a period of several years.

Whatever we see and do in our daily life may be so familiar to us that we rarely question it. But if our habitual viewpoints and actions don't work well for us — if they cause us repeated difficulties or emotional pain — then we may become interested in or at least curious about how we might be able to make some corrections. As important parts of our healing, we can accomplish that by sorting and owning what is ours and what is not ours, and by having healthy boundaries.

Projections as Boundary Invasions

In the previous chapter I described a way of defending ourselves against emotional pain: We may *project* onto other people unconscious aspects of our own inner life — unfinished business, feelings and experiences about which we may not be aware. Because they are too painful for us to experience and own, we perceive these traits, characteristics, feelings and patterns in others. In that way we keep at bay having to deal with our own pain, at least temporarily. When we do this, we are attempting one of the most complex kinds of boundary invasion, through which we will likely block our ability to have healthy and fulfilling relationships.

To heal a projection, I must first be able to recognize it. There are several *guises* under which I can begin to identify my projections (Table 7.2). These may include: the core issue of all-or-none thinking and behaving, strong reactions, repetition compulsions, limits or strengths in my own behavior, projective identification and resentments. Whenever I enact any of these, I am usually in one way or another disowning some aspect of my inner life and assigning or projecting it onto another person, group, place or thing.

When I project in any of these ways, I am *invading another's boundaries,* although I and they usually don't know this is happening. Whatever I am unconsciously projecting onto them and perhaps attempting to project *into* them not only *may* not be theirs, it is likely that it is *actually not* theirs. Rather, it is mine — only *I may not know it yet.* For one reason or another, I have unconsciously chosen to keep this material out of my full awareness. The advantage to my *knowing* and *owning* it is that by doing so I can eventually heal any woundedness that I may have around the projected material. Then I can be free of these often disabling associated projections. I name, own, experience, work through, learn from and let go of whatever it might be, and I thereby heal and grow.

Table 7.2 is on the next two pages, and I continue describing how to sort and own what is mine and what is not mine in the next chapter.

Table 7.2. Guises Under

Characteristic	Definitions
1. **All-or-None** thinking and behaving	Seeing people, places or things as only one way (which may be either positive or negative).
Conspicuously absent feeling or judgment [105]	Variations on all-or-none: What traits do I *never* see in certain others?
Idealizing or **disparaging** any person or groups	What traits do I *always* see in certain others?
2. **Strong "yuk" reactions**	A strong feeling of revulsion, antagonism or related emotions, usually in reaction to another's behavior. The reaction is often stronger in degree than is appropriate for the other's behavior.
3. **Repetition compulsion**	What mistakes or poor choices do I make over and over?
4. **Limits in my own behavior**	What things do I *never* do, even though doing them may benefit me?
5. **Strengths** in my own behavior [105]	What "strengths" do I have that, being preoccupied with them, may prevent me from being real and having fulfilling relationships?
6. **Projective identification**	What aspect of my inner life do I not want to experience and own, but instead may project onto another or others?
7. **Resentments**	Longstanding, unresolved anger or bitterness

*Such a reaction may also unconsciously remind me of another's neediness, which may have impacted upon me in a negative way in my past.

**Sometimes a resentment may be legitimate, and we may not be projecting; or it may be legitimate and we may also be projecting. This is where Table 8.1 may be helpful.

Which Projection May Appear

Examples	Possible Projected Material
All bosses are exploitive. All men are untrustworthy. All women are out to get men's money.	I'm exploitive, or I let others exploit me. I'm untrustworthy, or I trust people too easily. I have issues around money and giving.
University and college professors are never wrong.	I don't want to own my own intellectual capabilities.
All clergy are beneficent, helpful and trustworthy. All Germans are Nazis.	I don't want to acknowledge the clergy's dark side; or my own hurt and anger at Nazis' behavior.
I hate Joe's constant neediness. I hate "wimps."	I fear facing my own neediness, dependence or vulnerability.*
I keep getting into relationships that misunderstand and mistreat me. Or I keep doing other self-destructive behaviors.	I give aspects of my personal power away to other people, places, things and behaviors.
I *never* share one or more of my feelings or secrets. I *never* confront my ___ when they mistreat me. I *never* miss a day at work.	I fear dealing with the pain and joy of sharing, *and* of confronting my ___, *or* of being alone with myself and feeling vulnerable.
Always caretaking for others prevents me from caring for myself.	As stated in example.
See Table 6.1	As stated in definition.
I resent her for *fill in the blank.*	I may fear facing my own *fill in the blank.***

8

What Is Mine?
What Is Not Mine?
Sorting And Owning – *Part Two*

Working Through the Conflict

Rather than continuing to live in the pain of staying stuck in any of these kinds of projection, we can work through the *conflict* that is surrounding it. When we are in such a conflict, it can be useful to explore at least three levels of the conflict.

Three Levels of Conflict

1. **My Present Conflict.** The first is the most obvious — the conflict we have with the person or people in our life right *here and now*. Depending on several factors, the meaning of our differences with them may vary from minor to major in the actual dynamics of the particular conflict. But no matter what these are, we will likely have to somehow work through this level of the conflict to arrive at a resolution. If the issue exists *only* at this level, it should be relatively easy to resolve.

2. **My Past Unhealed Conflict(s).** The second level takes us deeper into our True Self, perhaps even into its unconscious, that part of us about which we are right now unaware. At this level our conflict may not be so much with the person(s) at Level 1, but with a person or people *from our past* with whom we have not been able to work through a prior conflict that is similar to the conflict in Level 1. At this level our feelings are intense and often overwhelming. Common sense resolution escapes us.

To help us become more aware of this kind of unfinished business, we might ask ourself the following question: "Of whom or what from my past does or might this conflict (from Level 1) remind me?" We might then tell someone safe or write our answers to this healing question. If we are reminded of anyone or of any specific experience, we can then begin to work on answering some of the following:

> With whom was the conflict?
> When was it?
> How old was I?
> What happened?
> What happened next?
> What happened after that?
> Did I ever try to resolve it? How?
> Is there any way for me to get free of this unfinished conflict?

In Table 8.1 I have made an outline of these levels and questions to use in helping to resolve these kinds of conflicts. Depending on the conflict, its duration and the others involved, it may take us days to weeks to months or even longer to work through an unfinished conflict. It is helpful to take as much time as we need. While there is often pain associated with it, there is usually no rush to resolve this conflict. If they are available, use your therapy group, therapist and/or journal to assist in your work around such a conflict.

3. **My Internalized Messages or Beliefs.** The final level may be still deeper. This includes painful material, patterns or messages that we may have stuffed or repressed into our unconscious mind which we may still believe about ourself (i.e., "old tapes"). These are usually related in some important way to the conflict in the first two levels and thus may also be important in resolving the conflict.

To help us become more aware of this level of our unfinished business, we might ask ourself the following questions:

- What rigid rules or negative messages did I hear or learn around this past conflict?
- What beliefs, belief systems or attitudes did I form around the past conflict?
- What aspect or part of the person(s) in this past conflict might I have incorporated or taken in as though it were now a part of myself?

We might then tell a safe person and write our answers to these healing questions in our journal or diary. As with the previous levels, we can use our group, therapist or journal to assist in our work around this level of our conflict. Table 8.1 shows an outline that may be useful in working through such a conflict. (Before writing on this chart, consider making some extra copies of it for use in helping to resolve future conflicts.) Remember that this two-page chart is not a final solution to resolving conflicts and transference issues. But it will often be a substantial help.

Continuing to Heal the Conflict of the Projections

Depending on the person with whom I am in conflict, how safe and available they are and how committed I feel to the relationship, I may or may not be able and/or want to work on this conflict directly with them. No matter what, I can work on it in group therapy, individual therapy, in my journal or in some other safe way.

Table 8.1. Checklist To Aid In Resolving A Conflict

Level of conflict	What is the conflict about?	What are my feelings and other Inner Life around the conflict?
1 With Person or People or Situation Here and Now		
2 With Past Unhealed or Unfinished Conflict		
3 Painful or Negative Messages, Material or Patterns Resulting from Past Conflict		

This is a lot of material to consider. Give yourself plenty of time to work through any of it. Anytime you wish, including when you have completed it, use extra paper to write about what this work may be bringing up for you. Take regular breaks from it, especially if you feel overwhelmed. Make extra blank copies of this chart for future use.

Some clarifying questions	Some possible answers, meanings and solutions to the conflict
Importance of conflict to me?	
Minor? Moderate? Major?	
What would it mean and/or result in if I were to resolve this conflict?	
What do I want to happen?	
What would I have to give up to get what I want to happen?	
Of whom or what does this conflict in level 1 *remind* me? Who was it with? When was it? How old was I? What happened? What happened next? After that? Did I ever try to resolve it? How? Any way to get free of this unfinished conflict now? How have I worked on this conflict in my therapy group, individual session or journal now?	
What rigid rules or negative messages did I hear or learn around this past conflict?	
What beliefs, belief systems or negative attitudes did I form around this past conflict?	
What aspects or part of the person(s) in the past conflict might I have incorporated or taken in?	
How have I worked on this conflict in my therapy group, individual session or journal now?	

It is our Child Within or True Self who does the work in resolving conflicts and in working through this kind of projection, which can also be called *transference*. It is generally our false self or negative ego that contributes to the formation of the conflict. However, that false self or ego may also be a "friend in disguise" *at times*, as it might be trying to tell us something important or help us survive what feels like an overwhelming or dangerous situation.

While there are no hard and fast rules about recognizing these kinds of boundary invasions that we call projections, those shown in Table 7.2 are some common examples. However, this doesn't mean that every time any of these examples occurs it automatically indicates the presence of an unconscious defense of projection. It may be that the current conflict (Level 1 in Table 8.1) is all that is there. Or it may mean that both Level 1 (the current conflict) and Level 2 (the past unhealed conflict) are each present in varying degrees. It may also be that the Level 1 conflict is not as important as the projection or transference that is manifested in Level 2. We can begin to differentiate these over whatever amount of time we may need to work it through.

Even though we may advance in our recovery as we form healthier and healthier boundaries, conflicts related to projection do not go away. Like the ducks in a carnival shooting gallery, unconscious material tends to keep manifesting itself in our lives. But the difference is that in advanced recovery the frequency of these conflicts tends to slow down and our ability to be aware of and to work through them tends to increase. We become able to identify and work through our projections, transferences and conflicts more easily and rapidly, as we bring our unconscious material more fully into our conscious awareness. As a result, we form more fulfilling, close and intimate relationships. These principles are illustrated in the following case history.

Jill had been divorced for seven years and had been in recovery as an adult child of a dysfunctional family for the past five years. In advanced recovery, she was now enjoying being in an intimate relationship with Tim. Eventually they decided to live together. Those first few months were difficult for her because during even the most casual exchange, she expected from Tim — and thus she was unconsciously tempted to project onto him — the old teasing insults or subtle humiliations from her prior marriage.

Jill said, "I thought I had talked this all out in therapy, but I still tensed up over the silliest things. One time I accidentally cut an electric cord when trimming the hedges in front of the house. I was sure when Tim saw what I had done, he would call me "Dummy" like my ex-husband did. Instead, he just told me where another cord was. I learned from that and a few other obvious exchanges that I still needed to own and grieve some of the mistreatment from my ex-husband in our old dysfunctional marriage. As I did that, I knew more about where I ended and Tim began. Then the best thing happened. I could finally see Tim for who he really is. And he's a great guy — gentle, kind, totally different from my ex-husband. If I hadn't learned about my inner life and worked on my own boundaries, I would have projected all of my old hurts onto him, and neither of us deserves that kind of pain."

By seeing herself and her partner more clearly, with fewer entanglements from her prior partnership, she experienced greater joy and fulfillment in her relationship. As we continue to sort and own what is ours, as we recognize and work through our unfinished business, we can take several additional effective actions. These include:

1. Getting help from safe others
2. Listening to them
3. Being humble
4. Being vigilant
5. Working through the conflict myself

Getting Help from Safe Others

Sorting all of this out doesn't usually occur easily or spontaneously. When we are embroiled in the middle of our own
conflict and pain, much of which may be unconscious to us,
the truth about what is actually going on in parts of our
inner life may not be readily available to us. This is why it
can be useful to obtain assistance from safe and skilled
others as we sort out our boundaries and other dynamics in
the process of our healing. While there are no hard and fast
rules regarding just who will be the most likely to give us
the most objective and accurate feedback about our conflict,
the following may be useful.

The first principle is that the people from whom we may
obtain assistance and feedback should be *safe*. We should be
able to trust them to be real with us and to have most of the
characteristics of safe people, as shown in Table 8.2. Safe
people tend to listen to you and to hear you. They accept
the real you and validate your experiences and other material that you may tell them about your inner life. They are
clear and honest with you and nonjudgmental of you. Their
boundaries are also appropriate and clear. They tend to be
direct with you and not triangle others into conflicts that
may develop between the two of you (see Chapters 13 & 14
on Triangles). Finally, they are supportive and loyal, and the
relationship with them feels authentic.

By contrast, *unsafe* people may not really listen to you or
hear what you are actually saying, although they may pre-
tend to do so. They may or may not make eye contact with
you. They often reject or invalidate the real you and your
inner life experience. They may be judgmental or false with
you. They are often unclear in their communications. Their
boundaries may be blurred, and they may often send you
mixed messages. They may be indirect with you, often triangling in another or others when they are in conflict with
you. Rather than being supportive, they may be competitive

and may even betray you. Overall, the relationship just feels contrived.

Table 8.2. Some Characteristics of Safe and Unsafe People

Safe	Unsafe
Listen to you	Don't listen
Hear you	Don't hear
Make eye contact	No eye contact
Accept the real you	Reject the real you
Validate the real you	Invalidate the real you
Nonjudgmental	Judgmental
Are real with you	False with you
Clear	Unclear
Boundaries appropriate and clear	Boundaries unclear, messages mixed
Direct	Indirect
No triangles	Triangle-in others
Supportive	Competitive
Loyal	Betray
Relationship authentic	Relationship feels contrived

Not all of these characteristics are absolute. For example, some people who make eye contact, listen to you and are supportive may still be unsafe. And a safe person may be unclear and even appear to be judgmental at times. However, over time, these characteristics and others may be helpful in differentiating who is safe from who is unsafe. Gradually, your perception and intuition will become clearer.

Listen to Others

If one person gives you feedback that you seem angry, they may not be accurate. But if *several* say so, it may very well be true and well worth considering. (Rarely, group perception may be off too.) This principle is one of many reasons why group therapy is so useful in helping us heal our woundedness, a part of which may be having unhealthy boundaries.

Jane was a 34-year-old legal aide who joined a therapy group for adult children of dysfunctional families. From the beginning, she expressed anger at many of the group members and the group leaders, usually because they "just didn't understand" how her "pain was different" from theirs. Whenever she behaved in this way, the other group members told her how angry she appeared to them and that they had not caused her anger. They suggested that its source was deeper and that she needed to keep looking for it.

It took nearly seven months of the group's setting healthy boundaries in this way for Jane to begin to realize that she was actually angry at her parents, who had mistreated her as a child and continued to mistreat her. In the past, during several years of individual psychotherapy, she had been unable to come fully to this realization. Hearing *several* safe people give her the *same* feedback was an important factor in her eventual ability to name, own and express (safely in group therapy) her anger at her parents.

Being Humble

Being humble, or having *humility*, is being open to learning about self, others and our Higher Power. It is a powerful aid in recovery from nearly any kind of woundedness. When I am humble, which is neither groveling nor being a doormat, I have let go of some of my boundaries in a healthy way, so that I can know and experience novel and possibly nourishing things about myself and others. By being humble, and thus open to what is both inside and outside of me, I may be better able to sort out and own just what is mine and what is not mine.

Being Vigilant

Many people who have been traumatized many times may experience the symptom of *hypervigilance*, wherein they are nearly always looking out for something hurtful or bad that may happen to them. A manifestation of post-traumatic stress disorder, this often bothersome trait may be transformed in recovery to a healthy ability to see accurately and be sensitive to self, others and God.

To sort out and own what is mine — and not take on what is not mine — through recovery and healing, I learn to shift my vigilance from my outer life to my inner life. If I feel angry, I know it. If I feel sad, I am fully aware of it. And if I feel joy, I am aware of that also. I do not push away or defend against what is real and necessary in my inner life. Rather, by remaining vigilant, I experience, own, work through, learn and then let go of whatever parts of my inner life that I may choose.

I Do the Work

No one else — no other person or persons — can sort out for me just what is mine and what is not mine. Neither can anyone else own for me what is mine. I have to do these things myself.

In the middle of a conflict, handling all of this and more may not be easy. It will usually be *work*.

Even though we do the work, others are there to assist and support us. We find safe, skilled and supportive others to accompany and guide us through our work. The paradox is that we cannot heal alone, *and* the only way we can recover is by our own internal resources. Those internal resources are the sensitive, vulnerable and powerful dimensions of the inner life of our Real Self. In their own imperfections, the other people who assist us may at times frustrate us to go deeper within and gently unearth and nurture that Real Self that has heretofore been in hiding.

Little by little, doing all of the work of recovery, we empower ourselves with skills to work through all of the above. We learn to set healthy boundaries and limits so we can own what is ours and not have to take on anything that is not ours. *Even so,* others may *still* try to project material from their inner life onto us. How might we prevent our absorbing and taking on what is not ours?

What Is *Not* Mine?

Whenever I am in a relationship and I experience a conflict, usually with painful feelings coming up for me in the conflict now, I can ask myself a simple question: "Is this mine?" True, the *pain* that I am feeling right now associated with this conflict is mine. But is that pain mine to *own?* And am I *responsible* for smoothing the others' pain over and making it all right for the other or others involved in this conflict?

Since a conflict usually involves the opposing wishes of one person against another, I can also ask myself: "Are my wishes, desires or expectations in conflict with another's?"

My guess is that before recovery a large amount of the pain associated with many of our conflicts is actually not ours — only we do not know it. And in many conflicts, even during recovery, we take on pain that is not ours. We may have learned to do that from our family and society of origin, an important part of which was learning to have and use unhealthy boundaries. With these unhealthy boundaries, we took on pain from others that was actually not ours.

Healing My Real Self

The key to both owning what is mine and letting go of what is not mine is in healing my Real Self, my Child Within. Being and living from and as the Real Me, I now know what is mine, because I now have a full awareness of my inner life and its dynamics. I also have skills to uncover my important unconscious material whenever it may be manifesting itself in some way in my life.

Healthy boundaries help me differentiate what is mine from what is not mine, as shown in Table 8.3. What is mine includes my *awareness* of my inner life, and all the *components* of my inner life as they come up for me from moment to moment, from second to second. Also mine is my *behavior* and finally the *responsibility* to make my life successful and joyful.

Table 8.3. What is Mine and What is Not Mine: Some Guidelines

What Is Mine

1. My awareness of my inner life

2. My inner life, including:
    my beliefs, thoughts, feelings, decisions, choices, and experiences
    my wants and needs
    my unconscious material

3. My behavior

4. The responsibility to make my life successful and joyful

Healthy Boundaries

What Is *Not* Mine

1. Others' awareness of their inner life

2. Material from others' inner life, including:
    their beliefs, thoughts, feelings, decisions, choices and experiences
    their wants and needs
    their unconscious material

3. Their behavior

4. The responsibility to make their life successful and joyful

But what is *not* mine includes all of these same components that come from other people — their inner life material and awareness of it, behavior and responsibility to make themselves successful and joyful. Neither are they responsible for making me happy.

What helps me differentiate these two — my stuff and your stuff — are healthy boundaries. My boundaries help me know who I am and know a whole lot about what is genuinely and spontaneously coming up for me.

Having Compassion

We live and function in relationship with our self, others, and our Higher Power. If we had only *rigid* boundaries, we would keep others out of large parts of our life and we might end up feeling isolated, empty and alienated. If we had only *loose* boundaries, we would let others invade our inner life so much that we would end up confused and overwhelmed with all of their stuff. With healthy boundaries we can be flexible, opening or closing them as is appropriate for our wants, needs and life.

Compassion is a feeling that is also an *evolved* and useful state of consciousness and being. In fact, it is one of our highest states of consciousness, probably second only to feeling Unconditional Love. But it can sometimes be difficult to differentiate true compassion from the simple and trapping passion of active co-dependence, where there are usually unhealthy boundaries.[112]

Have you ever been moved by someone's story? We feel a similar empathy and passion in both compassion and active co-dependence. But in true compassion we feel warm and caring and yet do not feel compelled to jump in and rescue, fix or try to heal them. We are still there for people if they reach out to us in any way; but we are secure enough in ourself not to try to use fixing them to fill our own emptiness (Table 8.4).

With the unhealthy boundaries of active co-dependence, focusing outside of ourself, we usually live in the range of discomfort from apprehension to misery. In compassion, with healthy boundaries, we may feel a bittersweet peace. Although this peace may have a painful edge, we can abide as we contemplate or sit with the other. It is almost as though we are sitting there in attendance with the other, while practicing the Serenity Prayer:

God grant me the Serenity
To accept the things I cannot change,
Courage to change the things I can,
And the Wisdom to know the difference.

Table 8.4. Compassion, Co-dependence and Boundaries

Characteristics	Co-dependence	Compassion
Trying to fix, rescue, change or control		
Ego attachment	Yes	No
Attachment to the outcome of being with the other		
Healthy Boundaries	No	Yes
Living as True Self connected to God		
Feeling	Apprehension to misery	Bittersweet peace
Focus	Outside of self	True Self, connected to God, with the other person

If we are attached to the outcome and try to fix or rescue the other person, we are not practicing compassion. We are in a more primitive state of consciousness that we can call *passion*. A way to help avoid such a complication and its resulting pain is to have and maintain healthy boundaries.

In compassion, we can thus empathize, be with and not abandon others, yet not take on their pain to our detriment. Being compassionate is an important answer to the some-times expressed concern that with healthy boundaries we may be somehow cold or neglecting to others. It allows us to be close or intimate with others and to care about them, without hurting ourself. Doing so also allows us to be there more fully for them, since we now have a healthy self.

What *Was* Mine Is Now *No Longer* Mine

After I *own* something from my inner life or behavior, can I then *let it go* and be *free* of it? This experience happens commonly in recovery. It is usually associated with letting go of painful feelings or other undesirable inner life material or behavior. An example follows.

> **Colin** was a 46-year-old married businessman who grew up in a dysfunctional family. His father and mother constantly shamed him growing up, so much so that he developed a low self-esteem that manifested itself in numerous areas of his life, including his relationship with his wife, close others and in his business. Unable to be assertive, and not experientially knowing his Real Self, he repeatedly let others take advantage of him, to his detriment.
>
> In recovery Colin slowly learned that this shame he had carried for so long was *not his*. It did not belong to him. It was his parents' and others' shame that they had projected onto him over his lifetime, up until now. But he couldn't let go of that shame until he accomplished several important things. First, he had to *name* it as shame, which took him many months of recovery work in group therapy, a self-help group, reading and writing in his journal. Then, and closely associated with naming it, he *owned* it and *experienced* it. He did what I call "getting down on the floor and wrestling with it." This means that he got to know his shame in an experiential way, intimately and thoroughly. He also shared it with his therapy group and other safe people.
>
> Next, and also closely associated with the above, he worked out just *where* his shame had *come from* — his parents and toxic others. Also during this time he was learning about healthy and unhealthy boundaries. And finally, he learned to *let go* of this shame that *was not his*. While this work included much more than this simplistic summary indicates, including much grieving of his old hurts and losses, this entire process took just over five years of working his full recovery program. The result was that he experientially knew who he was, felt good about himself and stopped letting others take advantage of him to his detriment.

Colin thus learned that what was *once* his was *no longer* his. He no longer needed to carry or own the shame of other people. Setting healthy boundaries, he gave their shame back to them.

Conclusion

Sorting out and letting go of what is not ours is often easier than sorting and owning what actually is ours. Perhaps paradoxically, to do this kind of letting go takes a firm background in learning to sort out and own what *is* actually ours. Having healthy boundaries is a crucial part of this entire process.

9
Healthy Boundaries And Limits

As I heal my Child Within — as I realize my True Self and begin to live *from* and *as* who I really am — I discover what healthy boundaries and limits are and just how they are useful to me. I have a progressively increasing awareness that a major function of healthy boundaries is to protect the well-being and integrity of my True Self.

And as I heal, I learn that healthy boundaries and limits are necessary in several crucial areas of my life. These include:

- **Self-definition** and **self-care**
- All aspects of **healing my Child Within,** including
  Being real
  Identifying and getting my needs met
  Grieving my ungrieved losses and hurts
  Working through my core issues and basic dynamics
- **Healthy relationships** — Boundaries protect my Child Within's reality in each of my relationships.
- **Realizing Serenity** — With healthy boundaries, I can then let go of some of my boundaries, as appropriate, and live in healthy relationship with myself, others and my Higher Power.

Healthy Boundaries

As a child, when we were mistreated or abused, our Child Within protected itself by going into hiding, often deep within the unconscious part of itself. As I recover and heal, I discover that my True Self needs to go into hiding less and less. I gradually learn that the safest person with whom I can let free — and be — my Child Within is *myself.* The next are safe others, fellow travelers in my recovery process. Also sponsors, counselors and therapists. And best friends and trusted others.*

I learn that with these people my True Self can come out and stay out, as long as it continues to feel accepted and safe. But at certain times, even with these safe people — and even with unsafe people — my Child Within does not want to go into hiding. This is because I feel more aware, powerful and creative when it is out, awake and alive.

Since I know that my recovery includes sensing and seeing progressively more possibilities and potential choices in my life, and then making healthy choices, I begin to see that setting boundaries and limits is a healthy choice. This is because the boundary or limit protects the safety and integrity of my Child Within so it can *remain* out, aware and alive, and not always have to go into hiding. Also, by setting healthy boundaries I can be free to make countless healthy choices about nearly any area of my life.

Some Characteristics of Healthy Boundaries

But how can I know when my boundaries and limits are healthy? Some possible criteria follow:

1. **Presence.** To have boundary health — and to sense the usefulness or non-usefulness of a boundary — a boundary

---

*For a further description of the True Self going into hiding, see page 57 (also shown on page 28 of *A Gift to Myself* and pages 27-29 of *Co-dependence — Healing the Human Condition*). For a description of safe people, see the previous chapter.

has to be present in my *awareness* to some degree. If it is not present in my awareness, then I may not be able to set it or, if I choose, to let it go.

2. **Appropriateness, based on my inner life.** This begins to delineate some useful reasons why I may need the boundary. I set the boundary or let it go based on what I am experiencing right now in my inner life. My inner life includes my beliefs, thoughts, feelings, decisions, choices, wants, needs, intuitions and more (see Figure 1.1). So knowing what is coming up for me in my life is crucial in my setting healthy boundaries and having healthy relationships.

3. **Protective.** The boundary is useful to help protect the well-being and integrity of my Child Within.

4. **Clarity.** I am clear about the boundary with myself and with the other or others with whom I am setting the boundary or limit.

5. **Firmness.** To get what I want or need, how firm do I want my boundary or limit to be? I am in charge of how firm I want them to be.

6. **Maintenance.** Do I need to maintain or to hold firm on a specific boundary or limit for a period of time, to get what I want or need? Or do I need to relax the boundary or limit to get what I want or need?

7. **Flexibility.** To get what I want or need, how flexible do I want my boundary or limit to be? To have healthy boundaries, I need also to be flexible — when appropriate — for my healthy, individual human needs and wants. To have healthy relationships, I need to *let go* of my boundaries and limits when appropriate.*

---

* For example, Lewis and Schilling[62] say that the ". . . self . . . boundary is best viewed as the interface between the individual and the environmental field . . . This interface is in constant motion. . . . it cannot be considered a static phenomenon, but rather a dynamic one extending across time and space" [outer and inner space, I add]. While I discuss the importance of flexibility and receptivity in boundaries throughout this book, I describe these characteristics in more detail in Chapter 17.

8. **Receptive.** Would it be useful or enjoyable for me to *loosen* the boundary a bit and let another person, place, thing, behavior or experience in?

In Figure 9.1 I summarize these eight characteristics of healthy boundaries.

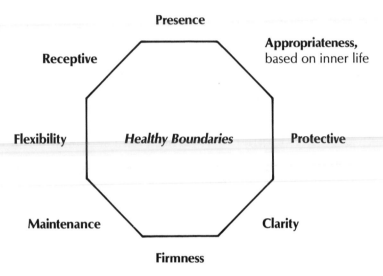

Figure 9.1. Characteristics of Healthy Boundaries

What Boundaries Are *NOT*:
Some *Un*-characteristics of Healthy Boundaries

Above are some characteristics of what healthy boundaries and limits *are*. But what are some characteristics that may help describe what they are *not?* We might call these some "uncharacteristics," because they are not characteristic of healthy boundaries.

Healthy boundaries and limits are *not:*

1. Set by any other or others
2. Primarily hurtful or harmful
3. Controlling or manipulating

4. A wall
5. Part of triangles with persons

Not Set by any Other(s)

Healthy boundaries are not set by others. I set my own boundaries and limits, according to and based on my own inner life.

It may take a while to learn this un-characteristic because throughout my life I may have had others tell me what to do or how to feel, (as illustrated in items 3, 13, 14, 18, 21, 26 and 36 of the *Survey on Personal Boundaries* in Chapter 2). And other people, such as those in my family of origin, and from whom I may have learned, may have modeled unhealthy rather than healthy boundaries for me to learn from. Some members of my family may still be influencing my life in a painful way, including doing so on *my boundaries*. As I recover, I can become more aware of all of these dynamics and begin to set my own boundaries by myself, wherein I can begin to let go of their pain that is actually not mine.

Not Primarily Hurtful or Harmful

Healthy boundaries are not primarily hurtful or harmful. I do not set out to hurt or harm another when I set the boundary, nor do I do so when I let go of a boundary. While it is not on purpose that I hurt or harm the other, my setting a boundary may nonetheless be painful to them. At times it may also be painful to me.

Two crucial questions in helping to sort this one out are: How hurtful to myself or to the other will it be in the long run if I do not set the boundary or limit *now?* If I don't set the boundary now, will my hurt and resentment build and eventually destroy our close or otherwise valued connection?

Not Controlling or Manipulating

Neither is setting a healthy boundary or limit controlling or manipulating of another. My definition of "manipulate" is when a person tries to influence or get something from another *indirectly*.

When controlling or manipulating, I am usually less aware — or perhaps even unaware — of my inner life. I may be invasive of the other, or dominating. All the while I may feel scared, ashamed, guilty or angry, and end up feeling drained or exhausted. I may end up feeling fused or enmeshed with the other, actively co-dependent.

By contrast, by setting a healthy boundary or limit, my purpose may include protecting the well-being and integrity of my True Self. I am aware of my inner life, and I am not usually invading another's inner life or outer life.

While I may feel any feeling in association with setting the boundary or limit, I usually feel comfortable. I may feel some discomfort setting them at first, and frequently so will the other. I am assertive, but not aggressive. I summarize these characteristics in Table 9.1 below.

Table 9.1. Some Characteristics Differentiating a Healthy Boundary from Needing to be in Control

	Healthy Boundary	**Control**
Purpose	To protect True Self	To control or manipulate
Awareness of Inner Life	Yes	Less aware or unaware
Invasive of Other	No	May be invasive or dominating
Feeling Often Associated	Usually comfortable, though may feel any feeling, including some discomfort at times	Fear, shame, guilt, anger; drained, exhausted
Other Dynamics	Assertiveness; healthy dependence and other dynamics	Fusion and enmeshment common; unhealthy independence and dependence

Not A Wall

A healthy boundary is not a wall (Figure 9.2). A healthy boundary provides me with my healthy human needs, which may include time and space where I can be alone — away from others, noise or other distractions. However, it does not wall me off from people, places, things and experiences unless I consciously choose *not* to be in relationship with them right now. An example of the latter would be a recovering co-dependent person who chooses not to be in relationship anymore with a toxic or dysfunctional person. Or a recovering alcoholic who chooses not to be in relationship with alcohol, not to take a drink or a drug, one day at a time.

Want to give me a hint what you're mad about?

Figure 9.2

By contrast, a wall is an unhealthy boundary. While it may have a useful and healthy purpose, the way I set it up and how it makes me and others feel may end up eventually hurting my own best interests. Some of the qualities of a wall are that it tends to be rigid, and the way that I set it up may be unclear to me and to others (Table 9.2). In close and intimate relationships, my wall won't let others in. I may lose some of my choices through its all-or-none characteristic. Often playing one or more roles unconsciously, I can experience and express little or no spontaneity. And despite all of my best efforts, I may end up feeling guilty, ashamed and afraid. A wall may involve disguised hostility and chronic mistrust, and is usually set up by the false self or ego, in contrast to the True Self, which sets healthy boundaries.

Table 9.2. Some Differences Between a Healthy Boundary and a Wall

	Healthy Boundary	Wall
Flexibility	Present, though may be firm	Rigid
Clarity	Present and clear	Often unclear
Lets Others In	Yes, when desirable and appropriate	No
Roles	Healthy, conscious, yet spontaneous as needed	Rigid, unconscious, with little or no spontaneity
All-or-None	No	Usual
Feel Guilt, Shame, Fear	Not usual, though may occur	Often
Set By	True Self	false self

Using a wall is in contrast to a healthy boundary, which, though firm, is flexible. It is based on my inner life, including especially my own healthy wants and needs. I am clear in how I make the boundary. If I am in a conscious role, I am also flexible and spontaneous as appropriate from my inner life and in my relationship. I expand my choices by working through being stuck in any all-or-none thinking and behaving that I may encounter. While I may at times feel some painful associated feelings, I can feel confident that I have acted appropriately, based on my inner life.

Once I have built walls, they not only keep others out, but they lock my True Self in. In an attempt to protect my Child Within, I have imprisoned it. As long as I maintain these walls, I won't know the Real Me, and neither will anyone else. Recovery is a way that I can bring down my walls, one brick at a time.

Not Forming a Triangle

A final characteristic of a healthy boundary is that by setting it, I do not form a triangle with a third person. Rather than forming triangles, setting healthy boundaries tends to prevent them.

I set the boundary with a single person at a time or with a single group at a time. I do not "triangle in" a third or a fourth person. I discuss triangles further in Chapters 13 and 14.

Conclusion

Healthy boundaries have several areas of usefulness. Learning about them in my recovery is crucial. I cannot recover completely without them.

Healthy boundaries have at least eight characteristics. They are: present, appropriate (based on my inner life), protective, clear, firm, maintaining, flexible and receptive.

Finally, healthy boundaries are *not:* set by others, primarily hurtful or harmful, controlling or manipulating, like a wall and part of forming triangles with others.

10
Relationships:
Their Basic Dynamics
And Boundaries

By now, you may have been reading this book and started to wonder what it would be like to be in a healthy relationship. You may even be ready to explore the possibility of having one now. You may even know of a particular person with whom you want to be in such a relationship.

Or you may already be in a relationship now, and be curious about how it developed in relation to boundaries and other interpersonal dynamics, and also about how to have a healthier self with healthier boundaries in this relationship.

Or you may be discouraged and skeptical as to whether you could ever have a healthy relationship. Yet you may want to explore this possibility more.

Whichever of the above situations you may be in, or if you are in some other one, it may be helpful to know about the following basic dynamics that can happen in the development, maintenance and enjoyment of any relationship.

Basic Dynamics in Relationships

While boundaries and limits are sometimes referred to as being an "issue," e.g., a "boundary issue," I find it helpful to describe them more accurately as being a *basic dynamic* in a relationship with any person, place, thing, behavior or experience.

During such a relationship, setting healthy boundaries and limits may be appropriate with *anyone*, at *any time* and *anywhere*. And *letting go* of them may also be appropriate, whenever I may choose.

These basic dynamics in any relationship often flow in the following sequence, which I list in Table 10.3 at the end of this chapter.

Need or Enjoyment versus Addiction or Attachment

Before I begin a relationship, I usually have a *need* for something about that relationship, or I may *enjoy* it in some way. The relationship may offer or may actually provide or give me something. Having a healthy openness to what comes up for me in my inner life in that relationship may help my not becoming attached or addicted to the person, place or thing. But if at any time during this relationship I do not maintain this healthy openness and balance, I may become addicted, attached or compulsive about the relationship.

Having healthy boundaries will help me to enjoy and get my needs met in the relationship and will help prevent my becoming addicted or attached to the person, place or thing.

Relationship versus No Relationship

Once having experienced getting something that I may want or need in a healthy way, if I want to go further, I can now choose to be in an early stage relationship. Or I can be in the relationship in a limited way, as described in *Intimacy or Closeness* below. Or I can choose *not* to be in any kind of relationship with this person, place, thing or behavior. Doing so is *always* my choice, at *any* time.

Bonding versus Bondage

If I choose to be in that relationship, I may then begin a process of healthy *bonding*. If I do not maintain healthy boundaries and limits and do not remain attentive to my True Self and its inner life, I could end up in *bondage*, actively codependent and feeling trapped, like a martyr or a victim. I discuss bonding further at the end of the last chapter.

By now you may notice that each of these basic dynamics is concerned with being aware of our inner life, with boundaries and with making choices. Each basic dynamic also has a healthy side and an unhealthy side.* It may demonstrate some other form of *opposites*, which may be further illustrated by the next basic dynamic.

Sameness versus Differentness

As the relationship continues to evolve, I may next encounter the dynamic of sameness and differentness. In my relationship I may notice what we have in common and how we are different. Sameness and differentness are important in my choosing both to continue and maintain the relationship — or to end it at any time.

Roles, Rituals and Habits versus Spontaneity and Flexibility

Eventually I may begin to notice that we are each taking on roles and enacting some rituals and habits. For example, when we get together, I may be the one who drives the car, and we may meet every Wednesday night for dinner. This can be healthy if both are *comfortable* and if there is a healthy amount of *spontaneity* and *flexibility* on both our parts. This allows us to vary our healthy roles, rituals and habits whenever it may be comfortable and appropriate.

---

* In any given relationship, it usually takes a while to sort out what is healthy from what is unhealthy for us. There is no need to hurry, so in your recovery give yourself plenty of time.

Having healthy boundaries and limits in the relationship, as in each of these basic dynamics, will help maintain a healthy balance of the two sides or dimensions of each specific basic dynamic.

Pursuing and Distancing versus Mutuality

In a healthy relationship there is an *equality* of pursuing and distancing by each partner. The other contacts me and initiates communications, get-togethers and activities about as often as I do. There is *mutuality.*[32,75]

In a less healthy relationship, I may do most of the pursuing and the other most of the distancing — or the reverse. Have you ever been in such a relationship? How does it feel to be relating in this way? What might your feelings and your observations about these basic dynamics mean about your participation in the relationship? Are you getting what you want and need in the relationship? To get what we want and need in any relationship, we can set healthy boundaries and limits, and we can also be assertive.

Boundaries and *Limits* versus Fusion and Enmeshment

Boundaries and limits are one crucial dynamic of these 12 basic dynamics in relationships. Figure 10.1 shows how they interact in an important way with each of the other eleven basic dynamics.

As an example, the following shows an interaction between the two basic dynamics of *boundaries* and *narcissism.*

> **Audrey,** a caretaker and people-pleaser, was married to Max, a self-centered rageaholic. Both were unrecovered adult children of unhealthy families. After three years of tolerating his repeated inappropriate behavior, which involved excluding her from decisions about their home and outbursts of rage at her when she tried to express her needs around all this, Audrey began therapy for her resulting frustration and pain. After six months of weekly individual

Figure 10.1. Interaction of Healthy and Unhealthy Boundaries with Other Basic Dynamics in Relationships

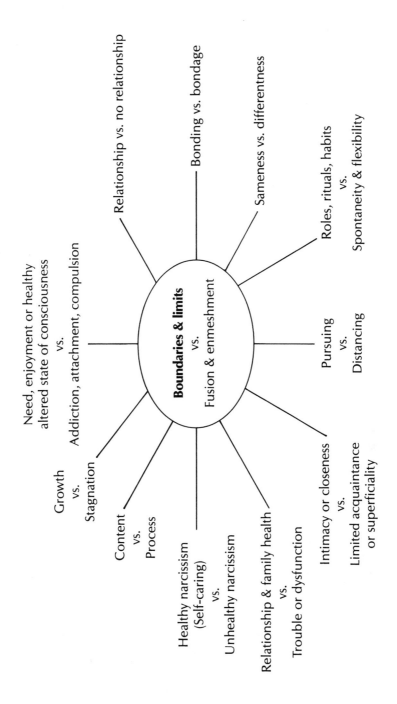

psychotherapy, she joined an adult child focused therapy group.

A year later she realized that her frustration was not only with Max. She was also enmeshed with her narcissistic, rageaholic father and with a narcissistic and shaming boss. Over the next year she began to care for herself further (healthy narcissism) by setting limits on all three. She told both her father and Max that she would no longer speak to them when they raged at her, and she became more assertive with her boss. While her puzzled and upset father kept his distance, Max had an affair and then reluctantly entered counseling with her. After eight sessions, half of which Max did not attend, she decided to separate from him — another healthy boundary.

Further work in group helped her discover that not only had she not been taught about healthy boundaries in her family of origin, but she had grown up in a mentally and emotionally enmeshed family. To survive, she made a false self that manifested in a caretaker role, which she had carried into her marriage and work.

After four years of recovery, she now has a strong sense of her True Self. Part of her continued self-caring (healthy narcissism) is using boundaries and limits to protect it. Still attending group therapy, she got herself transferred to another boss and is awaiting the finalization of her divorce in five months.

If I have a good working, experiential knowledge of healthy boundaries and limits — and of my True Self and its wants and needs — I will likely have used some boundaries and limits, consciously or unconsciously, by now in this particular relationship. And if I don't, I can now begin to learn about healthy boundaries and limits and how to use them constructively in my relationships and in my life. If I don't *experientially know* about boundaries and if I don't *use* them, I may end up fused or enmeshed in a relationship.

Fused or *enmeshed* means that my boundaries are blurred with yours. I don't know where I end and where you begin.

I may not be clear about just what are my feelings, wants, needs and other aspects of my inner life, and what are yours. I thus may not be an individuated (healthy individual) self in a healthy relationship with you. I may have lost my selfhood in you — and possibly in others — in an unhealthy way. I may feel afraid, engulfed, smothered, empty and lost.

Several other terms are similar to and may help further describe fusion or enmeshment: overinvolved, clinging, walking on eggs, over-responsible, needing to control, triangle, pushes buttons, high tolerance for inappropriate behavior, frustration, fear of abandonment, feeling obligated, can't say no, all-or-none, weighted down, stuck, resentment, taken advantage of, loose boundaries, rigid boundaries, unfinished business and repetition compulsion. In each of these states there is usually some degree of fusion or enmeshment. (I discuss fusion further in Chapter 13 on Triangles.)

Figure 10.2 is a cartoon illustration of a major factor in the genesis of *fusion* or *enmeshment*. We usually learn to lose our boundaries and limits in this unhealthy way from our family of origin, which this picture illustrates.

Figure 10.2. The Family Teaches Fusion

And what we learn, we can unlearn. As I heal my Child Within, I discover my blurred and unhealthy boundaries, my fusions and enmeshments. I notice them. Progressively, more and more often, I notice how I feel and how these and other unhealthy boundaries are associated.

If I choose to stop suffering unnecessarily, I can begin to set healthy boundaries and limits with others. I may now be discovering even more firmly that my healthy boundaries and limits serve to protect and maintain the well-being and integrity of my True Self.

Intimacy or Closeness versus Limited Acquaintance and Superficiality

Once I have a sense of *myself* and of *you* in our relationship — and of some of each of our wants and needs — I can continue to decide and to choose just *how close* I want to be.

An Intimate Relationship

Do I want an intimate relationship with you? I define an *intimate relationship* as one in which two people are *real* with one another *over time*. They dare to be vulnerable and to share their True Self with each other.[1] An intimate relationship works most successfully when both partners move toward realizing or actualizing their True Self, i.e., they are each healing their Child Within. While an intimate relationship requires risking and commitment, and can frequently be scary, it can also help us know and experience ourself and our Higher Power more fully and deeply. In an intimate relationship I will have to let go of my boundaries more often. At other times, when appropriate, I will set and maintain healthy boundaries and limits.

A *Close* Relationship

In a *close relationship* I may let down my boundaries and share with you, but not as much or as often as I would in an intimate one. In an intimate relationship I may share more dimensions of my life, including especially my inner life, than in a close relationship.

Mason (1988) has described nine life areas in relationships, as shown in Table 10.1 below. We can experience a closeness in any of these areas, and doing so can feel like an intimate *experience*. But that does not make it an intimate *relationship*. Mason says an intimate relationship exists when we have shared in at least four or five of these nine life areas with someone with the expectation that the experiences and the relationship will continue over time.[71]

Mason says, "Most of us have learned the cultural myth that we will meet someone special who will fill all our needs. But that would keep us dependent on others to fill us up. There is no one person who can meet all our needs; a healthy individual is one who can share a variety of experiences — with more than one other person. We need friends in our lives to support us and to walk with us."

Table 10.1. Life Areas that may be Shared in Relationships
(compiled from Mason 1988)

1. **Social** — sharing a group experience
2. **Intellectual** — sharing ideas or thoughts
3. **Emotional** — sharing feelings
4. **Physical** — working together
5. **Recreational** — sharing a recreational activity
6. **Aesthetic** — sharing what is beautiful or artistic
7. **Affectional** — sharing affection through touch or tenderness or special caring
8. **Sexual** — requires a prior relationship; deep closeness is possible
9. **Spiritual** — sharing a spiritual experience

I describe close and intimate relationships in more detail in my book in process on core issues and healthy relationships entitled *Wisdom to Know the Difference*.

Relationships and Family Health versus Family Dysfunction

We learn most about personal boundaries and limits from
our family of origin. Likewise, we tend to learn most about
each of the other basic interpersonal dynamics described in
this chapter from our family of origin. We also learn many
of these outside of our family, in our society of origin.

Most dysfunctional families model and teach unhealthy
boundaries. The more unhealthy, troubled or dysfunctional
the family, the more likely there will be distorted and unhealthy boundaries in each of the family members, including
each of the children.

> **Barbara** grew up in a moderately dysfunctional family,
> where, like most such families, the family norm was to be
> fused and enmeshed regarding personal boundaries. One of
> the main ways that her mother got attention, and at the
> same time tried to control and manipulate others, was to be
> repeatedly sick and have many medical and surgical proce-
> dures. At age 31, early in her recovery as an adult child of
> this dysfunctional family, Barbara — with the help of a hos-
> pital admitting clerk — set one of her first healthy bounda-
> ries with her mother. "I was irritable and depressed. I had
> withdrawn weeks earlier, after my third hospitalization. Be-
> sides traction, the chief of neurosurgery had performed a
> rhizotomy, a nerve block on my lower back, to try to stop
> the pain from getting worse. My doctor was highly respect-
> ed, a legend at Beaumont Hospital. My mother was also
> seeing him, and she was admitted at the same time I was for
> the same procedure. We laughed about the coincidence, but
> it seemed weird to me. My mother asked that we share a
> semiprivate room in the admitting office as I sat next to her.
> The woman behind the desk had said 'No' almost imme-
> diately. I was relieved. I knew I needed to take care of myself.
> No one knew what would happen, and I just didn't have the
> strength to take care of my mother now."
>
> As she describes in her books *Full Circle* and *Spiritual Aw-
> akenings*, over the next 16 years Barbara Harris continued to
> heal as an adult child and co-dependent. And as part of her

healing she learned to set healthy boundaries and limits, especially with her family of origin. This freed her to have healthy relationships with others.

Healthy versus Unhealthy Narcissism

Narcissism is focusing on my self and on getting my wants and needs met. It can be healthy or unhealthy. When healthy, we can call it *healthy narcissism* or *self-caring*. Without hurting another, we care for our healthy wants and needs in our own way and in our own time. And we do so by having healthy boundaries. We get what we want and need without invading another's boundaries and by setting our own healthy boundaries.

Unhealthy narcissism is focusing on self to the detriment of others. This detriment may be manifested and character-ized by a number of behaviors and dynamics, as shown in Table 10.2 on the next page. While some of these unhealthy traits may be present at times in ordinary active co-de-pendence, and while several may be present in other per-sonality disorders (e.g., borderline personality disorder), and in active addictions, *most* of them tend to be present in the psychodynamics and behavior of people with narcissis-tic personality disorder. Because of this association, the terms "narcissism" and "narcissistic" have taken on a neg-ative connotation, even though narcissism as self-focusing and self-caring can be healthy.

The person with unhealthy narcissism is acting the way our parents probably meant when they used the term *selfish* and told us "not to be that way." Yet what many of our parents didn't teach us was healthy self-caring. Before I can be in a healthy relationship, I have to know how to care for my self in a healthy way. Part of the way I can do so is by having healthy boundaries.

People with unhealthy narcissism frequently invade oth-ers' boundaries. Unless they work long and hard through an appropriate full recovery program, it is highly unlikely that

Table 10.2. Some Characteristics of Healthy and Unhealthy Narcissism[112]

Characteristic	Healthy	Unhealthy
Orientation	True Self	Negative ego
Humility	Present	Absent; ego inflated
Assertion	Self-assertive	Aggressive
Boundaries	Healthy	Unhealthy; often invades others' boundaries
Indulgence	Self-indulgent (as appropriate)	Selfish
Sees others	As separate individuals with own needs and feelings	Primarily as how others can be useful to them
Responsibility	Assumes appropriate personal responsibility	Blames others; avoids personal responsibility
Character defects	Owns character defects	Tends to project own character defects onto others
Needs to **control**	Values balance rather than control. Uses dominion rather than domination[57b]	Seeks to control or dominate people, places and things
Self-awareness	Self-aware (of needs and feelings)	Tends to be unaware (numb) or hypersensitive
Sensitivity	Sensitive to perceived criticism or rejection	Hypersensitive to criticism or rejection
Anger	Expresses appropriately	Inappropriate outbursts of anger or rage/or internalized rage and anger
Honesty	Tends to be honest	Often dishonest
Empathy	Feels and expresses	Lack of empathy
Flexibility	Realistic and flexible	Perfectionistic
Values	Values intimacy, love, productivity and creativity	Values "power," money, beauty and attention
Being around them is	Enlivening	Toxic and draining

they will change and become healthily self-caring. And so it is difficult, if not impossible, ever to have a healthy and fulfilling relationship with them.

Content versus Process

Content and process have to do with the communication, experience and reaction within any relationship. *Content* includes what words and sentences are said. *Process* is all other forms of communication that occur in the relationship, including our reactions, responses, behaviors and all other non-verbal ways of communicating. As with most of the basic dynamics, these may be used in either a healthy or an unhealthy way.

Regarding boundaries, each of these basic dynamics and the core recovery issues can interact with each other in various ways. For example, boundaries may interact with content and process at the level of the core issue of high tolerance for inappropriate behavior. This can be illustrated in the relationship of a married couple, Clay and Sally, both adult children and chemical dependent.

> **Clay** was in a full recovery program for his chemical dependence, and **Sally** was not. In fact, although she was ordered by the court to be abstinent from alcohol and drugs and to be in a recovery program, she was still drinking. She was so dysfunctional that she frequently called Clay from a bar or a friend's home at three in the morning to come pick her up and to pay for her drinking or drug-using bill, even though she knew he had to work the next day to support them. His boundaries were so loose that he tolerated this inappropriate behavior for over a year, picking her up and paying her bills. In spite of his occasional telling her of his frustration and hurt (content), his behavior (process) of not setting healthy boundaries and limits cancelled all his best-intentioned words.
>
> Clay required many sessions working in group therapy during this time to see what was happening and how his own

behavior was not only enabling Sally to continue being actively addicted, but was also endangering his own recovery and disrupting his life. He finally realized that his most healthy choice was to care for himself, and he separated from her. She moved in with her sister and continued to go downhill in her active addiction. While he was strongly tempted several times to get back together with her, with the help of his therapy group and AA sponsor, he was able to maintain these healthy boundaries and to grow in his own recovery as both a recovering chemical dependent and co-dependent.

I chose this story of Clay and Sally, an extreme example of disordered content and process, to illustrate them more clearly. Content and process in most relationships are less dramatic and more subtle. Because of this subtlety, it can be helpful to monitor what is going on inside you and in the relationship and to ask your partner if they would be willing to do the same. Indeed, because process can be so powerful and because much of it may go on inside our own heads, whether as fantasy or not, in any relationship it can be helpful to check in frequently about what may be real and what is not for each other. To do so may require risking, or opening a boundary, to bring up the particular subject or concern.

Growth versus Stagnation or Regression

When we heal our Child Within, our True Self, we grow. When we live from and as our True Self, we are free to explore, connect, reflect, learn, struggle, experience, create, celebrate, enjoy and just be. Healthy boundaries protect our True Self so it can stay out and be and do and experience all of these, thereby evolving and growing.

When our True Self goes into hiding and stays there, we cannot grow. Without healthy boundaries, our Child Within may be too scared or hurt to come out. And so we stagnate or regress. Instead of being and feeling like a Hero or Heroine, as described in Chapter 12 of *Healing the Child Within*, we may feel like a martyr or a victim, trapped and unhappy.

Discovering and using healthy boundaries can allow us to come out of hiding and be real, as our True Self, and to grow and experience serenity.

Conclusion

In this chapter I have briefly described some important basic dynamics in relationships, as summarized in Table 10.3. Being aware of, understanding and using these may help us make our relationships and lives more successful and fun.

Table 10.3. Basic Dynamics in Relationships

1. Need or Enjoyment vs. Addiction or Attachment
2. Relationship vs. No Relationship
3. Bonding vs. Bondage
4. Sameness vs. Differentness
5. Roles, Rituals & Habits vs. Spontaneity & Flexibility
6. Pursuing & Distancing vs. Mutuality
7. **Boundaries** & **Limits** vs. Fusion & Enmeshment
8. Intimacy or Closeness vs. Limited Acquaintance & Superficiality
9. Relationships & Family Health vs. Family Dysfunction
10. Healthy vs. Unhealthy Narcissism
11. Content vs. Process
12. Growth vs. Stagnation or Regression

11

Core Issues And
Boundaries – *Part One*

Core recovery issues interact with boundaries in numerous ways. When unhealed, these core issues impede and hinder our ability to experience and be our True Self. They ultimately block our ability to have healthy relationships with our self, others, and God.

The Core Issues

An issue is any conflict, concern or potential problem, whether conscious or unconscious, that is incomplete for us or needs action or change. A core issue is one that comes up repeatedly. There are at least 15 core issues:

- Fear of abandonment
- Low self-esteem
- Control
- Trust
- Being real
- Feelings
- Dependence
- Grieving our ungrieved losses
- All-or-none thinking and behaving

- High tolerance for inappropriate behavior
- Over-responsibility for others
- Neglecting our own needs
- Difficulty resolving conflict
- Difficulty giving love, and
- Difficulty receiving love.

How They Heal

Core issues reflect some of our areas of conflict as healthy human beings. They show up for us in our day-to-day lives in countless ways, especially in the following areas:

- **Relationships** — of any kind — with others, self and our Higher Power
- **Experiential** recovery **work** — throughout our healing
- **Feedback** given by therapy group members, therapists, sponsors, friends and others
- **Insight** from reading, listening, reflecting upon or working through conflict

Working Through a Problem, Conflict or Issue

The core-issues approach to recovery can help us apply an appropriate *name* to particular problems or conflicts. Once we name an issue, we can begin to focus on more of the essentials of our particular struggle. Once *focused*, we are less and less distracted by nonessentials and can thus concentrate on working to resolve the issue. To do this work of resolving an issue, we can use any of a large number of experiential techniques (see page 83).

Working It Through

As we name and work through a core issue, it can be most helpful to address it in a series of steps or stages.

1. Identify and name my specific upset, problem or conflict.
2. Reflect upon it from my powerful inner life.

3. Talk about it with safe people (that is, tell them that specific part of my story).
4. Ask for feedback from them.
5. Name the core issue.
6. Talk about it some more.
7. Ask for some more feedback.
8. Select an appropriate experiential technique.
9. Use that to work on my specific conflict and feelings at a deeper level.
10. Talk and/or write some more about it.
11. Meditate or pray about it.
12. Consider how I might learn from it.
13. If I still feel incomplete, repeat any of the above.
14. Whenever I am ready, let it go.

Boundaries and Specific Core Issues

To work through whichever of these core issues may be most important to me, I will likely need to set some healthy boundaries and limits. To set these boundaries, I can benefit by being in the company of *safe* people who will *validate* the truth of my shared experience. I will also need repeated *practice* at such sharing and at working through my core issues (Table 11.1). Finally, I will likely benefit from *guidance* from skilled helping professionals and others about how to go about the process of healing my True Self.

Boundaries can be categorized as being one of several *basic dynamics* in relationships. While boundaries are not usually considered to be a core issue, each of the basic dynamics interacts with each of the core issues in important ways.

As I work through my most meaningful issues, I may notice some important interactions between them and my personal boundaries. In the following, I give some examples of interactions for each of the 15 core issues. Because it is probably the most pervasive and primitive of all the core issues, fear of abandonment is an appropriate one with which to begin discussing boundaries.

Table 11.1. Core Recovery Issues in Stages

Recovery Issues	Early	Middle	Advanced	Recovered
1. **Grieving**	Identifying our losses	Learning to grieve	Grieving	Grieving current losses
2. **Being real**	Identifying our real self	Risking being real	Practicing being real	Being real
3. **Neglecting our own needs**	Realizing we have needs	Identifying our needs	Beginning to get our needs met	Getting our needs met
4. **Being over-responsible** for others, etc.	Identifying *boundaries*	Clarifying *boundaries*	Learning to set *limits*	Being responsible for self, with clear *boundaries*
5. **Low self-esteem**	Identifying	Sharing	Affirming	Improved self-esteem
6. **Control**	Identifying	Beginning to let go	Taking responsibility	Taking responsibility while letting go
7. **All-or-none thinking**	Recognizing and identifying	Learning both/ and choices	Getting free	Freedom from all-or-none choices

8. Trust	Realizing trusting can be helpful	Trusting selectively	Learning to trust safe people	Trusting appropriately
9. Feeling	Recognizing and identifying	Experiencing	Using	Observing and using feelings
10. High tolerance for inappropriate behavior	Questioning what is appropriate and what is not	Learning what is appropriate and what is not	Learning to set *limits*	Knowing what is appropriate, or if not, asking a safe person
11. Fear of abandonment	Realizing we were abandoned or neglected	Talking about it	Grieving our abandonment	Freedom from fear of abandonment
12. Difficulty handling and resolving conflict	Recognizing and risking	Practicing expressing feelings	Resolving conflicts	Working through current conflicts
13/14. Difficulty giving and receiving love	Defining love	Practicing love	Forgiving and refining	Loving self, others and Higher Power
15. Dependence	Identifying our dependence needs	Learning about healthy dependence and healthy independence	Practicing healthy dependence and independence	Being healthily dependent and independent

Source: *A Gift To Myself*

Fear of Abandonment

If I am afraid that you or others will abandon me, then a number of problems will likely develop for me and for our relationship. Having a substantial fear of abandonment will usually result in my inability to be my True Self with you and to set and maintain healthy boundaries.

Since my True Self is the only part of me that can know and set healthy boundaries, and since healthy boundaries protect and maintain the integrity and well-being of my True Self, these two — actor and action, being and boundary — work together to begin to heal each of my core issues.

We need, often want and sometimes crave authentic relationship. The relationship may cover a spectrum from being casual to close to intimate. If I am insecure in my self, if I do not know and live from and as my True Self, then the threat of the other's abandoning me may prevent me from ever beginning to set healthy boundaries. Living then from a false self, often with unhealthy boundaries, a number of other core issues may be set into motion and then may become aggravated, including the following.

Low Self-Esteem, Shame and Other Feelings

One of the next most frequent problematic feelings is low self-esteem and shame. After all, why would anyone abandon me unless I am somehow inadequate or bad? So when another leaves me, without a healthy self with healthy boundaries, I may feel not only inordinate amounts of shame, but I may also be vulnerable to taking on and absorbing any other person's *projected* shame that is *not mine.*

With few and sometimes no healthy role models, and with repeated invalidation and rejection of my feelings of fear, shame and other emotional pain, I may end up with the core issue of difficulty handling feelings in general. With overly rigid boundaries of keeping my feelings in, and overly loose ones of letting in others' painful feelings that are not mine,

I may end up feeling numb, which is an empty and painful absence of feeling anything.

Often fearing that the other person may abandon me, and with low self-esteem and shame, I am now more susceptible to being wounded around several other core issues. These include needing to be in control, high tolerance for inappropriate behavior and difficulty trusting.

Inflicting fear, shame, guilt and hurt onto another is an *invasion* of their boundaries. Likewise, when I feel anger, I may have recently had my boundaries invaded, and that feeling may be telling me about it. Even so, there is a fine line between the above and creating unnecessary pain for myself by feeling feelings that are inappropriate and unnecessary. These two poles can be difficult to balance, but working a long-term recovery program can help us do so.[114]

Control

I can keep all of my painful feelings partially at bay by trying to control them, you and others. To accomplish this I will do nearly anything, including manipulate, lie, betray and even give up my True Self. Manipulation is trying to get something indirectly, and I likely learned it from my family and society of origin. In manipulating and trying to control, boundaries are nearly always blurred and/or overly loose or rigid. I invade your boundaries or let you invade mine in an attempt to control you — or someone or something else. But except for a few things, like our bladder and bowels, control is usually an illusion. By trying to control life in this way, I often won't get what I want anyway.

High Tolerance for Inappropriate Behavior

To keep you from leaving me, I may loosen my boundaries even more, to such an extent that you can mistreat me. I will repeatedly allow you to mistreat me or others, in hopes that you won't leave me.

With an already low self-esteem, it may not dawn on me that I don't deserve to be treated this way. I don't deserve your hurtful, inappropriate behavior. Since I don't yet fully know my True Self and since I have mostly unhealthy boundaries, I may let you invade my personal space inordinately. Is there any limit to how badly and how often I will let you mistreat me?

Difficulty Trusting

Since it is likely that I was wounded by and learned most of the above areas from my family and society of origin, where the mistreatment probably started at an early age and was inconsistent and unpredictable, how can I ever learn to trust? If these are the kind of relationships that I have grown up with, how can I know any different? So I will probably find subsequent relationships with similar unhealthy qualities, where I will be repeatedly mistreated, all of which will enforce my difficulty trusting.

> **Karen** was a 40-year-old adult child of a dysfunctional family. She often felt loved by her father, yet he and her mother repeatedly teased and rejected her. It took her over a year to trust her therapy group enough to tell them of her repeated mistreatment as a child, including having been sexually abused by her father. She also spoke of flip-flopping between overly trusting (often too loose boundaries) and not trusting at all (rigid boundaries). By risking to share her Real Self and its inner life, including her painful memories, with the group and other safe people, she has slowly learned to trust in a more healthy way.

Trust is one of the most basic of the core issues because it is intimately linked with nearly all the other issues and is crucial for nearly all relationships. If I can't trust you in the most important areas of our lives, how can we have a relationship? If I can't know and trust myself and most of my inner life, how can I know if and when you or someone else may be mistreating me? How then can I set healthy boundaries? (Figure 11.1)

Part of trusting is *feeling safe.* Unless I feel safe with you and with others, I cannot trust you by sharing my True Self with you. If it is scary to let the real me be out with anyone, then how can even I get to know it? Healthy boundaries are important in recovery and in life because they let my True Self come out, in part by protecting its integrity and well-being. In all of these ways and more, boundaries are an important part of trusting.

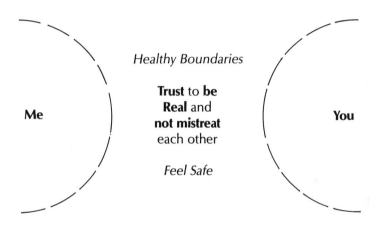

Figure 11.1. Boundaries and Trust

Dependence

If I can trust you, then that will help my chances of having a healthy dependent relationship with you. But even if I can't trust you, I still may need to be dependent on you in one or more ways, e.g., for finances and companionship. If I feel unable or unwilling to leave our relationship, I can use healthy boundaries to protect myself from being mistreated or abused.

But if I am a little child, totally dependent upon troubled, distracted or even toxic parents or parent figures, how can I survive unless I let down my boundaries and try to trust my parents? And so, through a series of traumas, I end up experiencing and learning unhealthy boundaries, unhealthy dependence and independence, as well as difficulty trusting.

A self-actualized or recovered person has a balance of healthy dependence within their relationships and healthy independence both within and outside of them. In their experience of healthy dependence there is appropriate closeness and sharing, and in healthy independence they have appropriate distance and privacy (gray area of Table 11.2). They have healthy boundaries.

Table 11.2. Spectrum of Boundaries and Their Relationship to Healthy and Unhealthy Dependence and Independence

	Unhealthy Independence	*Healthy Independence*	*Healthy Dependence*	Unhealthy Dependence
Boundaries	Inappropriately Rigid, Disengaged	Appropriate Distance and Privacy	Appropriate Closeness and Sharing	Diffused, Enmeshed, Fused
Description of state	Separated Isolated Alienated	— Healthy —		Martyr or Victim, Often an enabler
Live from	false self	— True Self —		false self
Co-dependent	Yes	— No —		Yes

By contrast, the person with unhealthy dependence on others has boundaries that are too loose or diffused, and are enmeshed or fused in their relationships. They may feel like a martyr or a victim and may also be an enabler.[112] A person who is unhealthily independent usually has inappropriately rigid boundaries and tends to be disengaged in the relationship. They often feel separated, isolated and alienated. Both tend to live from being attached to their false self and usually show manifestations of active co-dependence.

Grieving

Grieving is a painful but healthy part of our experiencing and healing of any hurt, loss or trauma. To grieve I have to know myself and trust myself enough to experience and release the stored energy of my pain over time. And I need safe others to be with me and listen in my times of grief. To grieve I also need healthy boundaries — first, to *let go of* so I can let my grief *out* and second, to *set a limit* if I'm around an unsafe person who won't validate my grief or who actively shames me for it.

12

Core Issues And Boundaries —
Part Two

Interaction among Core Issues

After having reviewed half of the 15 core issues and explored some aspects of how each of them may relate to boundaries, it may be useful to pause here and look at an example of how these core issues may interact with one another (Figure 12.1). I believe that fear of abandonment is the most appropriate issue with which to start this cascading interaction because it is so pervasive, primitive and powerful. It runs many parts of our lives, and through this kind of chain reaction it may erode our sense of self so much that we end up unable to be real most of the time. To be real, I need boundaries and to have healthy boundaries, I need to be real.

Before recovery, we may find it difficult to be real. And when we are not real, we usually feel empty and unfulfilled. During recovery I learn that the only way I can fill my emptiness and experience peace and joy is to realize my True Self and then experientially connect it to the God of my understanding. Working through my core issues as a part of healing my True Self will be a major factor in the process of my ongoing recovery.

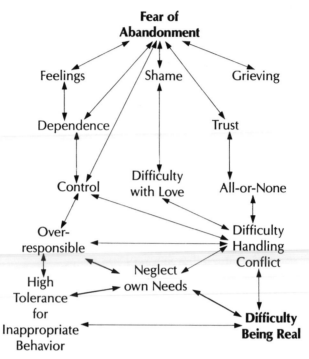

Figure 12.1. Inter-relationships among Core Recovery Issues:
From the perspective of **fear of abandonment,**
which ultimately may block **ability to be Real.**

All-Or-None

All-or-none thinking and behaving is also one of the first and most primitive of the core issues commonly encountered in any stage of recovery.[109,112,115] It limits my possibilities and choices because it says that all I can want or get in any relationship is "all or none." Either a *zero* or a *ten* — nowhere in between. But how often do I ever get "all"? If rarely or never, then what does that leave? None. So with an all-or-none mindset, I may end up with *no* choices.

We get stuck in all-or-none thinking and behaving when we remain attached to our false self. The false self can make only walls, not healthy boundaries. As I begin to live from and as my True Self, I can learn to set healthy boundaries and limits, which in turn will allow me many more choices in my life. Now I can choose among any one or more of the many points from zero to ten.

Difficulty with Love

Difficulty giving love and difficulty receiving love are two core issues that relate to boundaries in important ways. To let my love *out* and to let another's love *in*, I have to loosen my boundaries.

I also have love within me. But before I can discover the love that is in me, at the core of my being, I have to get to know who I really am (Figure 12.2). I get to know my True Self by peeling away the constricting layers of the false self and all the pain that I have made for myself by attaching to it. By protecting the integrity and well-being of the Real Me, boundaries allow me to come out of hiding and to heal and be myself. As I heal myself slowly throughout my recovery and my life, I experience the love that is already and always inside of me. I can then extend it outward, like rays of sunshine, to others and to God and God's domain. Doing all of the above also opens my heart to receive nourishing love from others and from God.[25]

Being Over-Responsible

Being over-responsible for others may give me the illusion that I can accomplish more than I actually can, such as controlling others. It may also give me the illusion that I am handling the conflict in our relationship in a healthy way.

> **Lil** was 32 years old, the daughter of Sam, age 60. He took care of her financially because, in spite of her intelligence and master's degree education, she could never find a job that suited her. As long as Sam took this responsibility for her, she had little impetus to work for a living. There was always tension between them.

When Sam began his own recovery as an adult child, he wanted Lil to work a similar recovery program, which she refused. It took him over three years in individual and group therapy to realize that his over-responsibility for her was enabling her not to take responsibility for her own life. He then gradually withdrew the money he was giving her. This was soon followed by her sudden marriage to a man 20 years her senior. She still is not working to support herself but Sam is learning to set healthy boundaries with her.

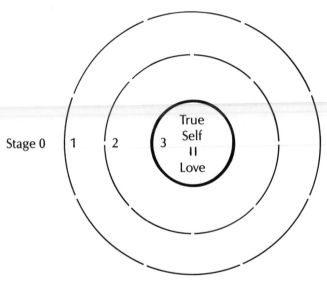

Figure 12.2. The Core of Our Being is Love
(I explain the stages of recovery in Chapter 15)

In working through the core issue of needing to be over-responsible for others, we first identify that we have a problem with boundaries (Table 10.1). We can next identify our boundaries, eventually clarify them, and then learn to set healthy boundaries and limits, as Sam was beginning to do. This leaves us better able to be *responsible for our self*, with clear boundaries with others.

There is often a delicate balance between the dynamics of *dependence* and *independence* in a healthy relationship and being over-responsible for others. [112] A way to begin handling this balance is to be real with ourselves and safe others and to monitor and experience our inner life, while having healthy boundaries and limits in our relationship.

Another manifestation of being over-responsible is trying to change, rescue or fix another. To handle any of these, we can use any of the above ways, and we can experience compassion for the other who may be in pain. (See Chapter 8, page 110, for a discussion of compassion and boundaries.)

Neglecting Our Own Needs

We each have healthy human needs, from feeling safe to authentic experiencing and communicating to feeling accepted and loved. [109] When I neglect getting these needs met for myself, I can become over-stressed and eventually overwhelmed, alienated from my Real Self. Preoccupied by people, places and things outside of myself and stuck in other unresolved core issues, I neglect my healthy self-caring. And I suffer as a result.

Part of the problem may be that here my boundaries may be too loose in certain areas. I may let in too much of other's toxic material, while at other times invading other's boundaries, all ending in neglecting my own healthy needs. When I neglect my needs, I tend not to set many boundaries at all. In recovery I learn to get my needs met in part by developing healthy boundaries.

Difficulty Handling Conflict

Difficulty handling conflict is one of the hardest core issues to heal. This is because being in conflict is so scary or upsetting. As adult children of dysfunctional families, having grown up with blurred boundaries all around us, we have not been taught healthy ways to handle the conflict of differences and disagreements.

Jim was a 50-year-old dentist who tried to handle conflict by withdrawing or running away. He learned this in his family of origin, where his father left the house at nearly every conflict that came up, often instigated by Jim's nagging mother. During his 30s Jim used benzodiazepines (Valium-type drugs) to handle his fears, and eventually became dependent on them. In recovery, drug free, he has begun to learn to handle his fears and conflicts by facing and experiencing them and sharing them with safe people, including his therapy group, his best friend and more recently with his wife. In his therapy group he learned not to run and hide. With the group, best friend and wife he learned that others will support him if he risks being real enough to share his feelings, wants and needs.

Part of the way that Jim learned to handle conflict in these ways was through having healthy boundaries. He set limits with unsafe people and found himself feeling progressively safer with his group, best friend and wife. And he let go of his walls enough to share many aspects of his inner life with these safe people. The result was that he became able to work through and resolve his conflicts as they came up for him, freeing himself to be real, be more creative and enjoy his life.

The act of *setting* a boundary or limit often leads to a feeling of fear and tension and, therefore, conflict. Likewise, *letting go* of a boundary can do the same. In the extreme of these feelings of conflict, we may age regress, which is a sudden state of confused, though strong, feelings which often leaves us feeling paralyzed. In age regression there is nearly always an actual invasion of our boundaries in the present — or a remembered one from our past, as I describe in Chapter 5.

Difficulty Being Real

Being stuck and unhealed around all of the above core issues, it is hard to be real. How can I be real if I don't know who I really am and if I don't feel safe enough to be real?

Healthy boundaries are one important ingredient in my being able to be real, to be and live as my True Self. This is because boundaries protect the integrity and well-being of my True Self.

When I am real, I can have almost unlimited potential in my relationships and my life. I can be aware of my inner life, connect with and relate to others in healthy ways, and heal any of my woundedness that I may wish. I can experience, learn, grow, celebrate and enjoy my life.

Conclusion

Boundaries interact throughout all of the core issues, and each core issue interacts with boundaries. As we heal our core issues, we learn about boundaries — what they are, how to set them and let them go, which are healthy and unhealthy, and when and how they are useful in our lives.

Boundaries interact with core issues — and core issues interact with each other — much more than what I have described in this chapter. Later in my recovery, when I have a healthy self with healthy boundaries, I can sort out and own my core issues and other unfinished business without projecting them onto others. This will allow me the freedom and ability to work through them faster and more completely — whenever they may come up for me.

13
Triangles

A triangle is an unhealthy relationship among three people. Whenever the pain of a two-person relationship becomes unbearable, one or both of them may bring in and involve a third person, place or thing to help relieve their pain. This forms a triangle, as shown in Figure 13.1. Healthy boundaries help prevent involvement in triangles and their painful consequences.

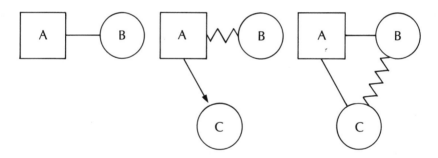

Figure 13.1. Common Dynamics in the Formation of a Triangle
(from Kerr and Bowen 1988)

The left diagram in Figure 13.1 shows a calm relationship in which neither person is sufficiently uncomfortable to triangle-in a third person, place or thing. The center illustrates the occurrence of conflict and unbearable pain. The more uncomfortable person, **A,** who also may be the less recovered or self-actualized, triangles a third person, **C.** The right diagram shows that as a result a substantial amount of the conflict and pain has transferred mostly out of the original twosome and into the relationship between **B** and **C.** [54]

An example: Mother, father and child are relatively calm. If mother and father have a conflict they cannot resolve, one of them may involve the child in such a way that their conflict and pain is transferred to an interaction between the other two.* Similar to what happens in projective identification, where one person avoids owning and dealing with their own inner life material, the formed triangle takes away the responsibility that the mother and father could take upon themselves to work through their conflict. This original conflict *did not belong to the child.* Yet by forming the triangle the parents are teaching their child unhealthy boundaries by modeling them. And they are wounding the child by forcing it to take on what is not the child's.

By contrast, in a healthy family, mother and father resolve their own conflict between themselves, even though they each may have to tolerate for a while the emotional pain that goes with it. By doing so, they teach their child healthy boundaries by modeling them and, when appropriate, by explaining what may be happening should the child appear concerned.

The concept of triangles is old: "Three is a crowd." They exist in all families and in all human relationships. The only question is the number, intensity and composition of the triangles in one's life. [32]

In recovery, which includes learning to set healthy boundaries, we can gradually discover how to identify and disengage from and sometimes even avoid getting involved in triangles. And the more recovered, self-actualized or differ-

---

* Involving the child in this way may also occur with the participation of both parents, usually through unconscious collusion.

entiated each of the three people in an old triangle may become, the greater the chance that they may even be able to change it into a healthier threesome.

A Threesome

A threesome is the interaction of three healthy two-way relationships (Table 13.1). Each member functions from their True Self, and thus with authenticity and spontaneity. While it is an open system with flexible movement among the three people, there is closeness or even intimacy experienced between each of the three pairs. The awareness of their own inner life by each member generally tends to be high, and boundaries are generally healthy. In fact, it is the healthy boundaries that assist in keeping the threesome intact, in part because they help keep the *two*somes intact.

Table 13.1. Triangle and Threesome: Some Differentiating Characteristics

	Threesome	Triangle
Condition	Healthy	Unhealthy
Definition	Three healthy two-way relationships interacting	An unhealthy three-way relationship
Awareness of our Inner Life by Each Member	High awareness	Low to absent awareness
Consciousness of Each Member	Mostly True Self	Mostly False Self
System	Open	Closed
Spontaneity	Mostly present	Usually absent
Movement	Flexible	Fixed, rigid or reciprocal
Interaction	Closeness	Fusion
Boundaries	Healthy	Unhealthy

However, most triangles cannot be transformed into a threesome because it is unusual for each of the three members of the triangle to go through a process of recovery to a sufficient degree at around the same time. Even so, if only one or two of the three recover, the frequency of triangular interactions and their detrimental consequences may decrease remarkably.

Triangles and Fusion

A triangle is thus an unhealthy three-way relationship. Each member functions mostly from their false self, with little spontaneity. It tends to be a closed system with fixed, rigid or reciprocal movement. While there may superficially appear to be closeness among the members, there is actually usually only fusion. In *fusion,* one person overlaps the other so that there is an indistinctness of self-identification or self-differentiation (Figure 13.2). What overlaps are usually aspects of the two people's inner life and behavior. It is difficult to tell what is self and what is the other person, and it is difficult to tell where self ends and the other begins.[32] We usually learn fusion experientially in our family of origin. (See Figure 10.2 and further discussion of fusion on page 131.)

Seeking the impossible goal of completeness and fulfillment through another person, place or thing, one person may:

- Try to merge into the other, in an all-or-none fashion, to gain self-realization. (I am right and you are wrong, or you are right and I am wrong.)
- Or two people will try to merge into one. (We always agree.)
- Or one person will lose their self in the other person. (I live for only you.)[32]
- Or one person will usually pursue and the other will usually distance, with little or no mutuality in their relationship.

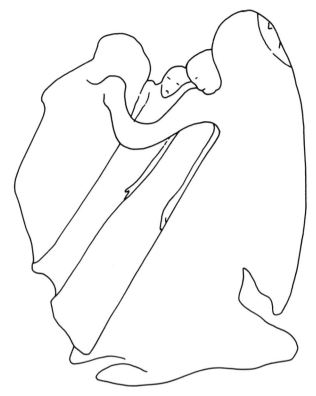

Figure 13.2. The Parents Enmesh the Children
(Drawing from Morand P et al: [The Art of]
Romaine Brooks, 1967)

When they get into conflict and the emotional tension
between them gets too high for either to deal with, one or
both of them may triangle-in a third person to lessen the
tension. In a triangle the awareness of their own inner life
by each member tends to be low to absent, and the boundaries of each tend to be unhealthy. The unhealthy boundaries prevent the autonomy and individuation required to
avoid the triangle, and they promote and maintain fusion.
Each person doesn't have a realized True Self from which to
be aware and to act appropriately, in part because they have
no healthy boundaries to maintain the integrity of their
True Self when it emerges.

The Origin of Triangles

The purpose of a triangle is to stabilize the two-person system when it is in danger of disintegrating. If two people can get interested in or distracted by a third person, object, issue or fantasy, they can avoid facing the real, threatening or scary issues between them. Ultimately, the triangle helps me avoid changing myself and my part of the problem.[32] By contrast, two people sharing in a common interest or activity in a healthy way or working through a conflict can nourish and enrich their relationship.

Triangles are learned from both inside and outside our family of origin. They are a product of how wounded and unrecovered or undifferentiated its members are. The more unrecovered the people are, the more important is the role of triangling for preserving emotional stability in a particular group of people. If there is relative calm, even in a family with very wounded and undifferentiated people, the three members of a triangle may function for a time as emotionally separate individuals. Since change and stress trigger fear and other painful feelings, more of these will tend to reactivate the active dynamics of the triangle. In a well differentiated system, such as a threesome, the members can maintain their emotional separateness and autonomy even when they are highly stressed. If people can maintain their emotional autonomy, functioning as their Real Self with healthy boundaries, triangling is minimal, and the system's stability does not depend on it.[54]

Triangles are often Complex

Stability

Triangles are not simple mechanical events, but are often complex interactions that have both personal (intrapsychic) and relationship (systemic) origins, dynamics, experiences and meanings. For example, the *stability* of any twosome can vary just by adding or taking away a third person, depending upon whether the relationship between the two is stable or unstable right now (Table 13.2). These examples illustrate the many potential guises by which triangles may present themselves in stable and unstable relationships. Note, however, that here "stable" does not necessarily mean healthy, nor does "unstable" always mean unhealthy. Note also that a fused or enmeshed relationship may destabilize at any time, since it is not usually made up of two recovered or individuated people having a healthy relationship.

Table 13.2. The Stability of a Relationship May Vary by Adding or Removing a Third Person
(compiled from Kerr and Bowen 1988)

If the Twosome is:	It Can be Destabilized by:	Example:
Stable	**Adding** a third person	Birth of a child in a harmonious marriage
	Removing a third person	No longer able to triangle their child, parents fight more after child leaves home
If the Twosome is:	**It Can be Stabilized by:**	
Unstable	**Adding** a third person	Birth of a child into a conflicted marriage
	Removing a third person	Two people avoid a person who takes sides on issues in their relationship, which foments conflict by emotionally polarizing the couple

Symptoms and Consequences

Other ways that triangles may show their complexity are by their symptoms, which frequently are also their consequences. Some of these may include:

1. *The original, unresolved conflict and pain* that wounds the person and thus predisposes them to be as involved in trian-

gles. Without realizing and living from and as my True Self — with healthy boundaries to protect and maintain its integrity — it will be difficult for me to avoid being involved in triangles to such a degree. This woundedness usually comes from growing up in a dysfunctional family of origin and society of origin, where triangles are universal. Most people grow up learning triangles, not healthy twosomes and threesomes.

2. *A lost, hurting self* then results from that original wounding. This can be manifested by recurring illness in any one or more of the physical, mental, emotional and spiritual realms of our life. Because our True Self is in hiding to survive, we come to rely upon our false self to run our life.[112] Not living from and as our True Self, we are left with the whims of the false self, which thrives on dysfunctional relationships, including regular involvement in triangles.

3. *Unhealthy boundaries* are both a basis for and a manifestation of being involved in triangles. Without boundaries and limits I cannot protect and maintain my Real Self that keeps me in healthy relationships and out of unhealthy ones, including triangles.

4. *Inner and outer confusion, pain and chaos,* usually with some interim periods of numbness and sometimes calm. A reduction in the frequency and intensity of this chaos and pain, as well as improved functioning in relationships, results from working through the long process of recovery.

5. *Repetition compulsions* may also be a symptom and a consequence of being involved in triangles. In fact, regular involvement in triangles is itself a kind of repetition compulsion. Repetition compulsions are making the same mistake over and over.

6. *Scapegoating* is identifying one person, place or thing in the triangle as being the victim or the problem. Underneath we can see that all three members are at the same time victim, problem and potential solution.

As Fogarty describes, "Father and mother may avoid marital strife by focusing on their son. That is one part of a triangle. Son and mother avoid facing the difficulties in their overcloseness by having a common enemy — father. Father and son avoid dealing with their distance by relating to each other indirectly through mother. There is no victimizer or victim . . . All members of a triangle participate equally in perpetuating the triangle and no triangle can persist without the active cooperation of its members".[32]

However, given two wounded and dysfunctional parents, the young child cannot inherently protect itself against their damage and come out unscathed. By triangling in their infant and child, the parents invade its boundaries and damage its Real Self, thereby wounding the child. In later life the child, now adult, can heal its woundedness by taking responsibility for its own recovery, in part by knowing these dynamics and then experientially working through the pain that they produced.

7. *Avoidance of closeness and intimacy* in a relationship where these would be appropriate is both a cause and a result of triangles. I can use healthy boundaries to help avoid triangles so I can focus on my wants and needs from my own inner life as I interact with my partner. Doing so promotes closeness and intimacy.

8. *Other symptoms and consequences,* including the creation of interlocking triangles.

Interlocking Triangles

Interlocking triangles occur when the pain of one triangle, unable to be contained, overflows into one or more other triangles. In a calm family, one central triangle can for a while contain most of its emotional pain. But under stress, this pain spreads to other family triangles and to triangles outside the family in the person's work and society. This process is illustrated in Figure 13.3.

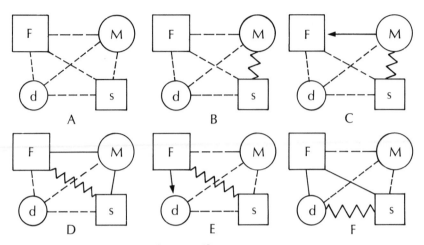

Figure 13.3. Diagram of a Family with a father, mother, older daughter and younger son. A: all the triangles are fairly inactive. B: tension develops between mother and son. C: father becomes triangled into the tension between mother and son. D: tension shifts to the father and son relationship. E. mother withdraws and the original triangle becomes inactive. Meanwhile the daughter is triangled into the father-son tension. F: conflict erupts between the two siblings. So tension originally present in one triangle is acted out in another triangle. (Modified from Kerr and Bowen 1988.)

Member Roles

The Pain "Generator"

In addition to the roles of scapegoat and victim mentioned above, members of a triangle often have rigid roles that tend to create the triangle, maintain it and keep themselves locked into the triangle. For example, some members may by their behavior tend to generate emotional pain in themselves and in the others, and can be called pain "generators." This "generator" or "persecutor" may set the emotional tone of many of the members, may upset people and may be the first person to get upset about potential problems, although they may not be the cause of that pain.[54]

The Pain "Amplifier" and "Dampener"

A second role is that of pain "amplifier," who adds to the problem through their inability to stay calm and stay out of the conflict if it doesn't belong to them. A third role is that of the "dampener," who uses emotional distance to control their reactivity to the others' behaviors. Under higher stress this person becomes overly responsible for others in order to calm things down. While the "dampener" may on the surface reduce some of its symptoms and consequences, he reinforces the creation and maintenance of the triangle.[54] We can also call this role "rescuer."

Abuser, Enabler and Other Roles

Other roles may also influence the dynamics of the triangle. These include the role of the "abuser," like the pain generator or persecutor, the most intimidating or dysfunctional one. Another is the "enabler," who unconsciously — and sometimes consciously — facilitates the destructive behavior of a dysfunctional person. This facilitating may include repeated attempts to rescue or fix the dysfunctional person.[112] Still other roles are those described by Wegscheider-Cruse and by Black: the family *hero* (responsible or successful one), the *scapegoat* (delinquent, acting-out or troubled one), the *lost child* (the adjuster or quiet one) and the family *mascot* or *pet* (little princess, Daddy's little girl or Momma's boy).[11,106] Each of these roles may add their own dysfunctional aspects to the rigid and stereotypical behavior of any member of a triangle.

Guises of Co-dependence

Since most people who are regularly involved in triangles tend to fit the description of being actively co-dependent, a member of a triangle may also play any of the roles that I described as being guises of co-dependence. In addition to some of the above roles, these may also include: people-

pleaser, overachiever, inadequate one or failure, perfection-
ist, victim, martyr, addicted, compulsive, grandiose and selfish or narcissistic one.[112]

Each of these as roles, guises or traits may bring different
aspects to the behavior of a member of a triangle. In recovery,
a person may draw upon any of these less desirable traits as
they transform them into healthier ones. For example, mar-
tyrs or victims can learn to be more sensitive to their inner
life and take responsibility for making their life a success,
which would include learning to set healthy boundaries.

With any three people, one triangle is possible. Add but
one more person, and now there are four potential triangles.
Add another for a total of five people, and there are eight.
By all of the above examples and dynamics in this chapter,
we can begin to see how common, pervasive, contagious
and destructive triangles may be.

Is there a way out?

14

Detriangling: Avoiding And Getting Out Of Triangles

Triangles are common, and avoiding and getting out of them is not easy. To avoid them we can take several actions, including:

1. Attain a *healthy self,* which includes
2. Being *autonomous,* individuated or self-actualized, both of which can lead to and benefit from
3. Having *healthy boundaries.* With all of these, we can keep on the lookout for involvement in triangles by having
4. An *awareness* of them when they are occurring or are about to occur. We can also
5. Learn and *develop skills* to detriangle, including
6. *Being real, being creative* and having *emotional autonomy.* Finally, we can institute all of the above by
7. *Taking action* to avoid or get out of the triangle.

Throughout all of this process is the underlying practice of *taking responsibility* for getting into a triangle in the first place and for getting out of it, as well as for owning all of my own inner life material as it comes up for me in each of the two relationships of the triangle.

In the previous chapter I said that triangles are not simple mechanical events. Rather, they are often complex interactions that have both personal (intrapsychic) and relationship (systemic) origins, dynamics, experiences and meanings. I also described several important relationship issues in triangles and will cover several more later in this chapter. But in the sparse literature that is available on triangles, there has been little written on their personal or intrapsychic aspects, which I will now describe.

Using Personal Material to Detriangle*

In Chapters 6, 7 and 8 I reviewed how personal or intrapsychic material — part of which can be called "unfinished business" — may interfere with having a healthy self. Exploring, owning and working through what is mine, i.e., healing my unfinished business, can enhance my having a healthy self. These principles are also useful to get out of a triangle, whether it is an old or a new one.

From this perspective we can illustrate the members of a triangle as being *myself* (shown as **M** in Figure 14.1), the person with whom I am in *conflict* (**C**) and the *wished-for helper*

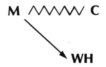

(**M** = myself; **C** = Person with whom I am in conflict;
WH = my wished-for helper)

Figure 14.1. My Inner Triangle

---

* The term detriang*ulate* may also be used and is synonymous with *detriangle*

(WH), the third member who I may unconsciously triangle in to help relieve the tension that I feel from the conflict.

Once I am involved in such a triangle, I can help myself by exploring what each of these three may represent for me within my own deepest self. In doing so, I may discover that as part of the triangle, *inside myself* (M) is a *conflict of dualities.* Each of the other two members of the triangle represents one of the two opposites in that particular duality (Table 14.1). For example, the person with whom I am in conflict (C) may remind me of my *"bad" parent* who prevents me from getting what I want or need. My wished-for helper (WH) may remind me of my *"good" parent* who helps me get what I want or need.

In other words, I go inside myself and into my past — *through* my present conflict — to tease out any parts of my having been wounded in the past. I can do this by using any of a number of experiential techniques, such as telling my story to safe people, writing in my journal or working through conflicts (also called transferences) in my individual or group therapy. I described some of these in Chapters 17 and 18 of *A Gift to Myself.* In this process I can also use the chart in this book (Table 8.1) on working through conflicts.

As I work through my being stuck in a particular triangle, I can consider several other aspects of my inner life to help me detriangle. These may include (Table 14.1).

- My *projections* (What parts of my unfinished business may I have projected onto the two others?)
- *Repetition compulsions* (Do I keep setting up these kinds of triangles?)
- My *awareness* of being in a triangle
- My *work* to detriangle
- The *responsibility* that I may take to work through all of this conflict.

Table 14.1. *Personal* or *Intrapsychic* Roles

Member of Triangle:	Myself (M)
Intrapsychic Representation	Conflict of dualities within my psyche, whether conscious or unconscious
Projection	I project aspects or parts of my unhealed inner life onto the two others
Repetition Compulsion	I keep setting up triangles . . .
Awareness & Work Before Recovery	I am not usually aware of most of this conflict
Wanting Help	I have to discover or remember that I am the one to work through my conflicts
Awareness & Work During Recovery	My job is to work through the conflicts in my *inner* triangle
Feeling Safe	I search for safety in my inner life
Related Core Issues (Examples)	**Feelings** Fear of **abandonment** Need to **control** **All-or-none** (dualities) **High tolerance** for inappropriate behavior
Detriangling	• Be real and objective • Work through my feelings • Set healthy boundaries • Can get help from a safe & skilled person outside the triangle
After Recovery	I have healed most of my conflict
Healthy Threesome	I work on myself, set healthy boundaries and include God.

and Dynamics in *Members* of Triangles

Person with Whom I am in Conflict (C)	Wished-for Helper (WH)
May remind me of my "bad" parent, etc.	May remind me of my "good" parent, etc.
I project the more painful aspects of my unhealed inner life onto this person	I project the less painful aspects onto this person
. . . in order to work through my conflict that this person represents	. . . or that this one represents, or both of them
This person may not be recovering/recovered & aware	Neither may this person
I would like something from this person, though I am not getting it	I ask this person for help, directly or indirectly
Provides the conflict	May or may not help me to resolve the conflict. May make the conflict worse
I feel less safe with this person	I feel safer with this person right now
They may have same or similar core issues	They may have same or similar core issues, plus being over-responsible
As during recovery (above) or after recovery (below)	As during recovery (above) or after recovery (below)
I will set healthy boundaries with this kind of person in the future	I (or we) will select only safe people and keep healthy boundaries, asking them more specifically what I want from them (e.g., just listen, give feedback, etc.)
I avoid closeness with toxic people	Same as under (M) and (C)

I can also consider how safe I may feel going into my inner life. At first I may be so unfamiliar with certain aspects of my inner life, such as my feelings, wants and needs, that it feels uncomfortable to go into it. And it is always uncomfortable to stay with or tolerate the emotional pain during any conflict. So a major part of recovery is learning to tolerate emotional pain while I work through my conflicts as they may come up in my day-to-day life.

When I *make the connection* between my present conflict and my past unhealed conflict in both an *experiential* and a *cognitive* way, I am then free to *grieve* and thereby release the stored painful energy from my original unhealed trauma. Doing so can assist me in eventually releasing myself from the triangle.

Using Boundaries

A major aid in detriangling is setting healthy boundaries and limits. When I am in a conflict with another person, I set my boundaries so that I do not triangle in a third person. If the person with whom I am in conflict tries to bring in a third person, I can likewise stay detached from becoming involved with them by maintaining my boundaries. Crucial to all of the above is having a healthy and autonomous self, which means that I am as fully aware as possible of and live from and as my True Self. It is because I have a healthy self that I can set healthy boundaries. This then frees me to focus on working through the conflict that I have with the other person.

If I find myself triangled into the conflicts of two others, I can likewise set my boundaries. Being the relative outsider, if I do not have a healthy sense of my self, or self-esteem, I may feel the need to try to fill my emptiness by getting closer to them through joining in their conflict. But it is at just this time that I can maintain emotional autonomy by working instead through my own issues, such as perhaps my now feeling like an outsider. Kerr and Bowen said, "Three people, together for a brief period of time, will invariably gravitate to a process of two insiders and one outsider. Well differentiated [recovered, self-actualized] people do not make a 'federal case' out of being an outsider, nor does their emotional security depend on being one of the insiders."[54]

Using Roles and Dynamics to Detriangle

Using the roles of *persecutor, victim* and *rescuer,* Utain describes the following dynamics in triangles.[102] Being vigilant for these may help us avoid or get out of them. Being my Real Self and having healthy boundaries are basic in detriangling.

1. A triangle tends to start with my not being real and honest.

   a. If I am dishonest with someone, whether it is about information, my feelings or experience, I may immediately enter a triangle.

   b. *Shoulds* will also pull me into a triangle. An important part of healing is learning how to go about getting my needs and wants met after learning to distinguish them from my shoulds or the things that other people have *told me* are my needs.

2. It *hurts* to be in a triangle. All positions in a triangle are painful.

3. There is *no personal power* in a triangle. No matter what role I am playing, I am operating from a lack of honesty and a loss of personal power.

4. Most people have a favorite starting role or position, usually rescuer or victim. Few initially choose to be a persecutor.

5. Like it or not, once involved in a triangle, most people end up playing *all three* positions. For example, I may have perceived myself as a rescuer who wound up as someone's victim, while at the same time that person perceives me as being their persecutor.

6. *Guilt* and other *painful feelings* tend to hook me into a triangle.

    a. When I feel guilty it is a signal that someone is attempting to pull me into a triangle.

    b. To stay out of the triangle, I can give myself permission to feel guilty without acting on it. In other words, I do not let the guilt push me into any of the roles.

    c. Thus, I learn to be uncomfortable and sit with the guilt.

    d. Other painful feelings, such as fear, shame and anger may likewise hook me into a triangle. I work through them also.

7. The *"escape hatch"* out of a triangle is often located in the *persecutor* position. Being real, telling the truth and feeling my feelings opens the escape hatch out of the triangle. To stay out of or to leave the triangle, I have to be willing for the other two to perceive me as the bad guy. This does not mean that I am the bad guy. But the others may choose to see me that way. If I am not willing to be seen as a persecutor, I will likely get hooked into rescuing and put myself back or keep myself in the triangle. If I am already in the triangle and want out, I may have to be willing for the other two to see me as the bad guy or persecutor.

In the process of leaving the triangle, I am beginning to be more aware of my inner life, including my feelings, wants and needs, plus my motives around being in the triangle. Open to being my Real Self with healthy boundaries, I am willing to experience my feelings and to let others experience their feelings without having to rescue them. If the other people in the triangle are willing to experience their feelings and to tell their truth, the triangle will likely dissolve. If they are not, as is more common, then I may leave looking like the bad guy.

8. I can also play triangles out *alone* — by myself. Raised in a dysfunctional family, I may not need another person to push me into a triangle.

a. Playing a triangle by myself happens when I listen to the negative voice inside my head that beats me up, puts me down and constantly *shoulds* me. These old tapes usually come from a dysfunctional family and society of origin. This *should-er* is my false self.

b. Remember, *shoulds* are *untrue*. They have nothing to do with who I am, who others are or how healthy relationships work. They are someone else's interpretation of what to do and what is "good" or "bad."

c. When I play a triangle with myself, my *should-er* will persecute me so that I will feel like a victim. At the same time I will be feeling guilt, fear, shame and/or anger. These may trigger the belief that I am the persecutor and drive me to rescue someone (or some situation), even when listening to my old tapes is what is trying to manipulate me into the rescuer position.

9. When I actively participate in a relationship with someone who lives in a triangle, I can be *vigilant for hooks*. It is difficult to be around people who constantly operate in triangles and not get hooked into them, especially if my personal boundaries are not clear and I have not learned to recognize triangles.

10. My internalized *should-er* is also the voice that pushes me into a triangle when the other two members are attempting to hook me. As my *false self*, the should-er is the part inside me that stores my old tapes but that I may mistakenly believe is me. It is negative, rigid, controlling, perfectionistic and self-righteous. Unattached to this false self, I would likely not participate in a triangle.

11. Being in a triangle is not being fully alive. It is a kind of living death. It is a life of inauthenticity, pain and lack of acceptance and love.[102]

12. *Being real* — telling the truth and experiencing my feelings — with *healthy boundaries* — is a way out of the triangle. To do that I have to learn to know and define my boundaries and take responsibility for recognizing, expe-

riencing, expressing and completing what comes up in my inner life appropriately with safe people — and sometimes with unsafe people.

We can consider and explore whether there may be ways to apply some of these principles to experiencing being in other roles in triangles.

The Relationships

Even with the above information I do not have to discontinue my relationships with these two people or divorce myself from them in order to detriangle. Indeed, if I choose, I can still relate to either or both of them in a healthy way. Relating in a healthy way involves establishing a relationship with each person separately, with each relationship having its own integrity and unique character, rather than developing an *alliance* with either person *against* the other. But by having a healthy self with healthy boundaries, I am better able to sort out just what is mine and what is not mine, and not get involved in or take on their conflicts. The ability to be in emotional contact with others, yet remain autonomous in one's own emotional functioning, is the essence of the concept of differentiation.[54]*

We can get involved in triangles with members of our family, friends, acquaintances, bosses or supervisors, colleagues

---

* While Bowen and his colleagues have used the word "differentiation" as a major concept in their theory and work, Bowen himself never fully explained the term. He did say that poorly differentiated people have a high percentage of life problems, such as physical and emotional illness, social maladaption and failures. Well differentiated people's thinking and feeling functions are more differentiated and autonomous; they have fewer life problems, are more successful in life, have more energy to devote to their own life courses, and their relationships are more free and intimate. Basic level of differentiation describes, among other things, functioning that is not dependent on the emotionally driven process of being in a relationship.[54] Although he had initially hoped that the general population would be distributed evenly over a scale of poorly to well differentiated people, he concluded that about 90% of them were in the lower half and perhaps 10% of them were well differentiated.[13] My sense is that Bowen's idea of "well differentiated" is nearly the same as "self-actualized" and close to what we would call being in an advanced level of Stage Two recovery (described on page 193 of this book and page 36 of *Co-dependence*).

and peers, teachers, spouses, lovers or others. Perhaps the most common situation is where I am already in a relationship with two others and a conflict develops between two of us. At that time either of us may triangle the third into our conflict, or the third may enter spontaneously. The third may also not be a person, but could be a pet, idea, ideology, cause, place, thing, behavior, group or another object.

Watching for Other Dynamics

There are four additional dynamics that may occur in a triangle: a *power difference, role reversal,* being in a *double bind* and *secrets.* Each or a combination of these may either draw us into a triangle or make us feel stuck in one. Knowing about them may prevent both.

Power Difference

In a power difference, one or two of the members have some kind of power over the other member or members that can be destructive to each individual and to their relationships as three people. For example, two parents have power over their child, who is vulnerable to their behaviors and whims. With this difference in power, unless the parents are themselves healthy or recovered, there is little likelihood that the three can have a healthy three-way relationship. Or a boss has two employees, and when they become triangled, her power as boss may clearly influence their relationships and the triangle. Of course, the child and the employees may have their own forms of power, which may set up still more variations within the triangles.

As we recover, we learn that there are different kinds of power. Moving from its most primitive to its most effective and sophisticated, at the lower end is power as *physical strength,* which can also include financial influence. Next is power as *manipulation* (maneuvering to get things indirectly), followed by *persuasion* and then *assertion.* These are all used by the parents and the boss above, and to some extent even by the child and the employees. These are the lowest levels of power.

But depending on the circumstances, there may be more effective kinds, including *watchful waiting* (the *Wu-wei* of Taoism), then *accepting* and then *letting go.* When I truly let go of something that is toxic or not mine anyway, I no longer beat myself up about it, thus freeing me to experience a more successful and enjoyable life. Continuing to the top of the spectrum of power, the next most powerful is *wisdom,* then *compassion* and finally the most powerful is *unconditional love.*[25,110,111]

Each of these various kinds of power, from the most obvious and primitive to the most sophisticated and effective, may be used at different times to get out of a triangle once in one, and to avoid getting into one if doing so can be anticipated. In employing each of these, we claim and use our personal power. We reclaim our personal power through a process of increasing awareness and by taking responsibility for our well-being and functioning: Power = Awareness + Responsibility. And part of that power is by setting healthy boundaries and limits.

Role Reversal

In a role reversal one person in a relationship takes on parts of another's role that should not belong to them. The child attends to Daddy's needs over the long term, when the reverse should occur. Unable to have a healthy intimate relationship with her mate, his wife may collude with the child. The child becomes the caretaker to the parent, as the parent places his needs above the child's. Yet the parent does not give up control. In his narcissistic and manipulative way, he also often plays the child off against his mate. Even though the child is unable to be a child, she feels chosen and special, at times a variation on "Daddy's little girl," and tries always to be "good." Which of these set up and maintained the original triangle? Daddy's narcissism? Mother's distance?

Both parents' woundedness? Probably all of these did, as shown in the principle of unconscious collusion described in the footnote on page 160 in the previous chapter.

As the girl grows up, some of the destructive *consequences* of this triangle become more pronounced in her life. She becomes "depressed" when she is unable to care for her father, does not know her Real Self, is over-responsible for others in many of her relationships and cannot function in a healthy twosome or threesome.

To get free of such a triangle involves a long process, which I describe as Stage Two recovery (see page 191).[112] A crucial part of this healing will include naming what happened to her (some of which may be: mistreatment, triangulation, role reversal and lost selfhood) and then experientially realizing her Real Self, which will include coming to have healthy boundaries.

Double Binds

In a double bind there is no safe or healthy place for a person to go. They are damned if they do and damned if they don't. The child in the above family triangle is in a double bind. If she continues to give to her father while sacrificing herself, she will lose her selfhood. But if she speaks up for her needs, her narcissistic father, for whom she can never do or be enough, will shame her and her mother will likely guilt her. She is caught and cannot leave. As an adult, knowing this information and these dynamics can help her in her total recovery.

Double binds often originate in a family or other setting where the child in actuality cannot leave the setting and does not have the cognitive or emotional capabilities to formulate a solution within the setting. As the child grows into adulthood, they may continue to perceive — and through repetition compulsions to recreate — situations in which there are no safe alternatives for resolution.

Double binds are common in triangles, and they always contain an implied threat. Persons caught in one are usually abandoning themselves by inappropriately letting down their own boundaries and compromising their needs. Because most people who become regularly and strongly involved in triangles are not yet recovered enough to be able to recognize that they are in a triangle and how to get out of it, being stuck in this kind of situation is hard to deal with. Asking for help from a safe, skilled therapist can be a start.

Secrets

Another dynamic in triangles is having one or more secrets. One or two of the members may have a secret which may influence the triangle in some way. It could even be used as a point of "power" at times. But secrets are usually destructive to the individuals and their relationships.

A secret is anything we are told not to tell, or anything important that people may keep from one another. There are two kinds of secrets: healthy and toxic. Keeping a toxic secret can be damaging to us and to others. It may lower our self-esteem, increase our guilt, block our ability to grieve our losses and hurts (which may be part of the secret), and weaken our immune system. In short, it may block our serenity.

A healthy secret is a *confidence.* It is private. If we keep that secret and do not tell it, we will not be harmed, and neither will anyone else. By contrast, if we keep a toxic secret, or if someone keeps an important secret from us, we may be harmed. The point is not that we have to go out now and tell all of our secrets or even someone else's secret. What tends to be most healing and helpful for us in detriangling is that (1) we come to know any important secrets that may have been kept from us, and (2) we tell to a *safe* person any toxic secret that may be harming us — or that may harm them if they do not know the secret. (See Chapter 13 of *A Gift to Myself* for experiential exercises around secrets.)

Secrets tend to produce triangles. In a boundary violation, critical knowledge or behavior (the secret) may be kept from another. This withholding of information gives the secret-holder an unfair advantage in the relationship. A person with a secret can take on the illusion of thereby having "power" over the other two. If he tells one of them (the colluder) the secret and not the third member (the outsider), he has set up a triangle through these actions. In a boundary violation secrets may either (1) separate one or two of the members of a triangle while deceitfully maintaining the pretense of a common endeavor, or (2) superficially join the two who know the secret against the outsider.[88]

Keeping the secret is toxic to all three members of the triangle because it destroys trust, conceals information that the other(s) may need to know and erodes the relationship. Because the keeper(s) of the secret so often act out of *the secret*, rather than from their True Self, they may withhold an important part of or a potential point of communication, closeness or intimacy in their relationship. Sometimes the real secret is not about the content of the information but rather about the motive or intent of the keeper(s) of the secret.[88] All of these dynamics tend to stabilize and maintain the triangle.

For obvious reasons and because of their nature, secrets are among the most difficult for the *unknowing* person to deal with in any relationship, whether it be with only one person or more people. To help in detriangling it is helpful for the unknowing person who suddenly discovers an important secret which has been kept from them to work through their shock and pain in a constructive and healing way. Part of this healing will likely include sharing the secret and their feelings about it with safe people.[116]

For the *knowing* person(s), secrets are also difficult to deal with, though in a different way. Should they decide to help themselves detriangle by telling the secret, they will likely have to handle their resulting feelings of guilt, shame and fear, in addition to lost trust from the previously unknowing person. Deciding to tell and telling is a delicate balance. It may also harm the unknowing person or others, as the Ninth Step of the Twelve Steps addresses. Also, sometimes not knowing a secret can actually be more harmful than knowing it, although it may be painful to tell it and to know it. But should they decide not to tell the secret, they may still have to live with those feelings *long term*, in addition to always having to remember and watch what they say to the unknowing person.

In triangles, one or more of these dynamics is often present. They may interact, and they may aggravate and maintain the triangle. And when the present triangle is unable to contain all of the pain of each of its members, it may spread to and interlock with one or more other triangles.

Using Spirituality

While we have a relationship with our self, others and, if we choose, our Higher Power, whenever we are involved in any relationship we usually somehow also involve each of these three basic relationships. In this chapter and the previous one I have focused on the first two: our relationship with ourself and with others. But there is a third relationship that we can use, if we choose, and that is with the God of our understanding. After I have done everything that I know to do to avoid or get out of a triangle, I can also ask my Higher Power for assistance.

These two actions — doing what I can do and then letting God do the rest — are the components of the process of co-creation. (See the final chapter in *Co-dependence*.) While I can ask for this assistance and turn over whatever it may be that I need help with at any time in this process, it is most helpful if I have also done all that I can do first. I can ask and turn over all this remaining pain through prayer, meditation or any way that I may like to commune with God.

Conclusion

While they may offer some relief to the tension between two people who are in conflict, triangles also distract the two from working through it, in addition to all of their consequences described in the previous chapter. With the knowledge and skills contained in this book and elsewhere, we can now be strengthened in our ability to have healthier relationships and to begin to avoid becoming involved in unhealthy triangles.

15
Stages And Process Of Recovery

Learning to set healthy boundaries and limits is a crucial part of recovery. But trying to set or let go of them alone, without healing my True Self, may end up not being very useful for me. In this chapter I will review the stages of recovery, provide an outline of its process and show where boundaries fit into it all.

The Stages of Recovery

While boundaries are useful in all of the stages of recovery, it can first be useful to define each stage in sequence.

Stage Zero

Stage Zero is manifested by the presence of an active illness or disorder, such as an addiction, compulsion or another disorder. This active illness may be acute, recurring or chronic. Without recovery, it may continue indefinitely. At Stage Zero, recovery has not yet started (Table 15.1).

Stage One

At Stage One, recovery begins. It involves participating in a full recovery program to assist in healing the Stage Zero condition or conditions. (A partial recovery program is less likely to be as successful as a full one.)

Table 15.1. Recovery and Duration According to Stages

Recovery Stage	Condition	Focus of Recovery	Approximate Duration
3	Human/Spiritual	Spirituality	Ongoing
2	Adult Child	A C Specific Full Recovery Program	3-5 years
1	Stage Zero Disorder	Basic-Illness Specific Full Recovery Program	½ to 3 years
0	Active Illness	Addiction, Compulsion, Disorder ———————— Woundedness	Indefinite

When to focus on Stages 2 and 3 recovery usually depends upon the person's prior healing and present condition.

Stage Two

Stage Two involves healing adult child or co-dependence issues. Once a person has a stable and solid Stage One recovery — one that has lasted for at least a year or longer — it may be time to consider looking into these issues. An adult child is anyone who grew up in an unhealthy, troubled or dysfunctional family. Many adult children may still be in a similar unhealthy environment, whether at home, in one or more relationships or at work.

Stage Three

Stage Three recovery is spirituality and its incorporation into daily life. This is an ongoing process.

Boundaries are useful in Stage One recovery according to the disorder or condition from which one is recovering. For example, the recovering alcoholic will need to set a boundary by abstaining from alcohol and other psychoactive drugs, one day at a time, and by avoiding high risk "people, places and things." The person with migraine headaches will need to avoid factors and stresses that may trigger a headache. And so on.

By Stage Two recovery, while these boundaries still apply, the person is working on deeper areas of their life, such as the wounding that they experienced from growing up in a dysfunctional, troubled or unhealthy family and society of origin. One term that has helped in our ability to clarify and understand the relationship among these stages, the various disorders that may befall us, and the human condition is *co-dependence* — which is a disease of lost selfhood. It is during Stage Two recovery that we address this wounding and its manifestations, which we call the *adult child syndrome* and co-dependence (see Figure 15.1).

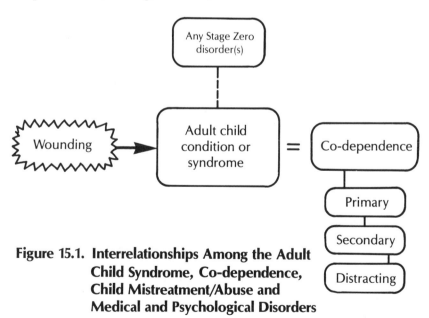

Figure 15.1. Interrelationships Among the Adult Child Syndrome, Co-dependence, Child Mistreatment/Abuse and Medical and Psychological Disorders

Most co-dependence is primary in that it occurs from childhood, as described in the wounding process discussed at the end of Chapter 4. Primary also means that no other disorder in the co-dependent person causes it, although one or more disorders — including addictions — may exist concomitantly.*

Figure 15.1 describes any of these disorders that may exist with co-dependence as "Stage Zero disorders." The Stage Zero condition or disorder represents the tip of the iceberg, with the bulk of the iceberg being co-dependence or the adult child syndrome. Depending on genetic, familial and environmental factors, each person will likely manifest a different Stage Zero disorder or set of disorders.

A person who obtains specific treatment for the Stage Zero disorder is now in Stage One recovery, which usually takes a few months to a few years to stabilize (see Table 15.1). In Stage One, *any* addiction, compulsion or related disorder may be addressed. Once stabilized, the person may wish to address the underlying co-dependence (which in perhaps 95 percent of people with co-dependence is the same as the adult child syndrome or condition). This Stage Two recovery usually takes from three to five years or longer in the best full recovery program. In Stage Three recovery the person is then more able to address and realize their spirituality.

The Recovery Process: Peeling Away the Layers of Co-dependence

One way to view the process of recovery is to compare it with peeling away the layers of an onion. Each layer is a manifestation and consequence of the false self and our attachment to it. And each layer surrounds, constricts and imprisons our True Self, the core of our being.

---

* The following material is selected and condensed from *Co-dependence: Healing the Human Condition*, which contains more details on the process of Stage Two recovery.

There are three layers. The first consists of the numbness, pain and confusion that are but a part of the many
foggy manifestations of the second layer. Until we cut
through this often nebulous first layer, we are still in Stage
Zero recovery, which is no recovery at all.

The second layer that binds our True Self consists of
addictions, compulsions and various other disorders. To pene-
trate any of these usually takes from many months to several years of working in a Stage One full recovery program.

Underneath this layer is the third and final layer: adult
child wounding and perhaps its major manifestation, co-
dependence. This layer contains a lot of fear, shame and
anger, three painful feelings that we have to deal with in the
long and exciting process of Stage Two recovery.

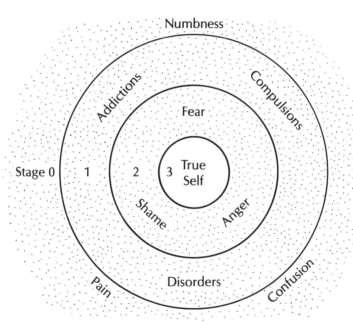

Figure 15.2. The Constricting Layers of Co-dependence

We can also call these three constricting layers manifestations and consequences of our attachment to our false self
(Figure 15.2). Underneath all of these layers, at the core of

our being, lies the goal of recovery and our true identity: our True Self.

We peel away these layers throughout the entire process of recovery. The work of peeling away each layer involves recognizing, addressing, experiencing and healing multiple problems and concerns, called "unfinished business." While I described some of the influences of and approaches to handling Stages Zero, One and Three here and elsewhere, my focus in this book is on the unfinished business of Stage Two recovery, and especially the usefulness of healthy boundaries. Finishing this business includes the following areas of recovery work: grieving, original pain work, working through core issues, doing "personality" work, completing developmental tasks and setting healthy boundaries.

These kinds of recovery work interact and merge with one another. They are not necessarily distinct or separate areas of the healing process. Figure 15.3 shows a Venn diagram of their relationships.

Grieving

Unresolved grief festers like a deep wound that is surrounded by scar tissue, a pocket of vulnerability ever ready to break out anew. It stifles our aliveness, creativity and serenity. We need three elements in order to grieve our ungrieved hurts, losses and traumas:

1. Skills about how to do the grief work
2. Safe and supportive others
3. Enough time to complete the process

An important part of grief work includes what can be called "original pain work."

Original Pain Work

"Original pain work" is a term that helps us describe and heal a particular acute and deep part of our ungrieved hurts. It greases the wheel of the grieving process and is an

**Figure 15.3. Key Areas of Recovery Work: Venn Diagram
of Their Interrelationship**

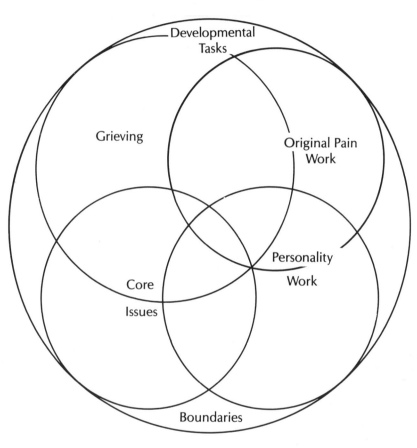

Personality work includes all work, plus working through transferences
as they come up.

important part of the grief work. Like grieving and recovery in general, this process cannot be forced or rushed, or
our Child Within will likely go deeper into hiding. While
there are many approaches to facilitating original pain

work, the following eight actions can help in this process and are examples of some of its components in an effective healing sequence.

1. I tell the story of my current upset to safe and supportive people, for example, in my therapy group or in individual therapy.
2. I cognitively and experientially connect my current upset, conflict and feelings around them to my past. To help with this process I can ask myself, "What does any of this current experience remind me of?" and then begin to answer.
3. I may write about it in my journal or in an unmailed letter. Or I may work through this conflict and its emotional pain by any of several other possible experiential techniques.
4. I bring in and read my unmailed letter (or describe whatever else I've done experientially) to my therapy group or therapist. I may also enact parts of the resolution of my original pain with these safe people, such as by using further experiential techniques (for example, gestalt or psychodrama techniques facilitated by my therapist).
5. In the company of these safe people, I then discharge the stored toxic energy until I feel as complete with it as I can for now.
6. Then I listen to feedback from the therapy group or therapist.
7. After listening to each person's feedback, I describe how my doing all of the above feels now.
8. I connect any future upsets and conflicts with what I have learned above.

Doing this original pain work can be an important stimulus to grieving our ungrieved hurts, losses and traumas. However, by itself this original pain work is not sufficient to complete our grief work, which usually requires several years to complete. (I will say more about grieving in "Essentials for Recovery" below.)

Working through Core Recovery Issues

I describe some basic principles of working through core recovery issues in Chapter 11 and in *A Gift to Myself.*

Doing "Personality" Work

The terms "personality" and "character" should not be equated with an individual's identity. While we are each unique and individual beings, as represented by the many aspects of our True Self, I believe that nearly all of the unhealthy and destructive aspects of our personality are due to a combination of our being wounded and to our attachment to our false self. Because these are so deep and unconscious, it takes some special work with a specially trained and experienced therapist to help heal them. Doing "personality" work means healing the results of our prior wounding. Even when these are influenced or caused by constitutional or "genetic" factors, I have observed that it is most conducive to the healing process to approach them as being nearly all due to wounding.

Some Therapist and Group Tasks in "Personality" Work

Personality work is complex. It requires trust and surrender on the part of the recovering person and experience and skills on the part of the therapist. This work is described in part in several books.[20,41,56,73,78] A helping professional who wishes to learn it will require clinical supervision by an experienced therapist. While using this work is not to be taken lightly, the following brief description may be helpful in providing an overview and outline of part of this process.

1. The therapist — and in the case of group therapy, the group — empathically connects with the person. This connection is important throughout their ongoing relationship.

2. The therapist (and group — with the facilitation of the group therapist when needed) accompanies and guides the person while working through their unfinished business.

3. The therapist recognizes the presence of transference (projecting emotionally-charged material that was acquired in the past onto others in the present), related core issues and any "stuckness" in developmental tasks, and assists the person in working them through. When we over-react — that is, react beyond what is appropriate for the situation or circumstances — this is a sign of transference. While transference can be dramatic in presentation, it is more often subtle. For example, transference occurs when we see and expect or experience the therapist or other as being an ideal parent while forgetting their human inadequacies; or when we attend to the therapist or other to please them, while neglecting our own healthy needs.

4. In such situations the therapist's constructive responses may include one or more of the following actions:

- Listening to and tolerating any projected material, while empathically connecting.
- Questioning (infrequently and only when appropriate) with such questions as : "What might this conflict remind you of from your past?" and "Can you let yourself experience whatever feelings are coming up for you right now?"
- Facilitating movement in any constructive way.
- Supporting the person's needs as appropriate.
- And (rarely or seldom) interpreting a particular and appropriate dynamic or connection.

In group therapy if the group member appears to be transferring onto one group therapist, the co-therapist steps in and facilitates the group member's work through the conflicts and the transference.

5. By using constructive feedback, the therapist (and other group members) validates, mirrors and supports the person during the work.

6. The therapist and other group members, as appropriate, set *healthy boundaries*. These boundaries and limits, coupled with a therapist who does not talk too often or too much, help provide the person with a healthy amount of frustration that helps to fuel working through the unfinished business.

7. The group and the therapist(s) provide the recovering person with new, safe and healthy interpersonal experiences that are part of the "grist for the mill" of recovery work.

Healing the personality's woundedness includes all of the work of recovery, plus the specific work around working through transferences as they occur. For a therapist to be able to provide healthy and skilled work requires a training experience of appropriately supervised work assisting many people over a duration of several years, as well as having completed a substantial portion of their own recovery as an adult child.

Completing Developmental Tasks

The work of completing developmental tasks is exacting and requires a working knowledge of the stages, issues and tasks of healthy and unhealthy human development. When appropriate, the therapist gently guides the person through these developmental stuck points.

Setting Healthy Boundaries

As I describe throughout this book, learning to set healthy boundaries and limits is a crucial part of recovery.

Summary

Figure 15.4 graphically summarizes some of the components of the process of peeling away the layers of co-dependence that surround and constrict our True Self. This illustration also shows how most of recovery is experiential, while some important parts of it are cognitive and behavioral. In my experience each of these usually involves each of

Figure 15.4. The Interaction of Key Areas of Recovery Work with their Cognitive, Experiential and Behavioral Components

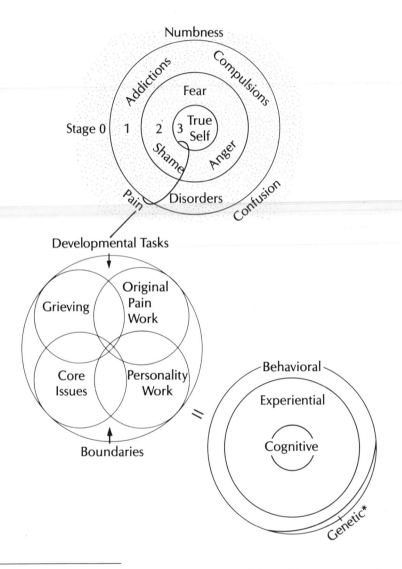

---

*Genetic Factors are more important in Stages Zero and One and less important in Stage Two recovery.

the others — e.g., the behavioral usually has both cognitive and experiential components.

Essentials for Recovery

At least twelve essential actions will usually make recovery go more smoothly and successfully:

1. Handling any distractions to recovery
2. Learning to live from our inner life
3. Learning about our feelings
4. Learning about age regression
5. Learning to grieve and grieving
6. Learning to tolerate emotional pain
7. Learning to set healthy boundaries and limits
8. Getting our needs met
9. Experientially learning and knowing the difference between our True Self and false self
10. Working through our core issues
11. Learning that the core of our being is Love
12. Learning to be a co-creator.

Let's look at each of these. A few of them are so important that I also discussed them in the previous section.

Handling Distractions

Learning to handle distractions includes identifying and stabilizing any Stage Zero disorders or conditions through working a Stage One full recovery program, so that we will be free to begin to know and heal our True Self. If we do not handle these distractions, they may prevent our ability to focus on our adult child and co-dependence healing.

Learning to Live from our Inner Life

In co-dependence we focus on our outer life to an unhealthy degree. In recovery we learn to focus on our inner life (Figure 1.1) so that we can more successfully live and enjoy our life, including interacting with others.

Learning about our Feelings

Feelings are a major and crucial part of our inner life. To learn about them, we usually have to "get down on the floor and wrestle" with each feeling. When we do that, we get to know them so well that eventually we will be able to do any of the following for each feeling: recognize it, feel it, experience it, work it through, use it, and then let go of it.

A particular feeling at a particular time may be either useful or useless, and it may even end up hurting us. Until we can recognize, feel, experience and work through a feeling, no matter how painful, we cannot use it and then let it go. [112,116]

Learning about Age Regression

I have described some important principles of learning about age regression in Chapter 5.

Learning to Grieve

Learning to grieve is crucial. When we grieve our un-grieved hurts, losses or traumas to completion, we get free of their chronically painful hold on us. A major part of recovery is about grieving.

As we work through grief, we first learn specifically what hurts, losses or traumas we have experienced. Then we begin to grieve them. Then we grieve some more, all the while learning progressively more about each of our feelings as they come up for us. Once we have grieved these major losses to completion, which usually takes several years, we are free to be our True Self and to grieve any current hurts, losses or traumas as they may occur. Then we tend not to become stuck in them, as we may have been in our past. [109,112,116]

Learning to Tolerate Emotional Pain

Learning to tolerate emotional pain helps us to stay in our present discomfort long enough so that we can work through it and learn and grow from it. Sometimes people become so frustrated that they flee their particular recovery aid. A more constructive choice is to stay in the pain and ask for assistance from safe others, such as a therapy group, therapist, sponsor or best friend.

Learning to Set Healthy Boundaries

I describe this essential action for recovery and life throughout this book.

Getting our Needs Met

Learning to meet our healthy human needs is also crucial in the process of healing co-dependence. These needs include the physical, mental, emotional and spiritual aspects of our being. We *get our needs met* as we grieve, experience and live our lives *in three relationships:* with our self alone, with safe others and, if we choose, with our Higher Power (see Figure 15.5).

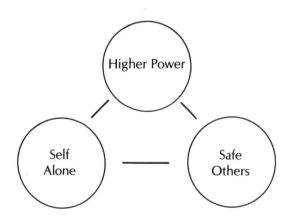

Figure 15.5. The Three Basic Relationships in the Healing Process

Learning the Difference Between True and False Self

In recovery it usually takes a long time to learn experientially the differences between our True Self and our false self. We can begin to explore this cognitively by looking at some of the differences, as shown in Table 15.2.

In 1985, when I began writing *Healing The Child Within*, I found it helpful to call the false self by another name, the co-dependent self, because the false self is the major "actor" and pretender in co-dependence.

The observer self is an important part of our True Self, the part of us that watches everything dispassionately and nonjudgmentally. When we step back into our observer self, we begin to notice some more important differences between our True Self and our false self. In any conflict the false self wants to be separate, rational and logical, and it wants to avoid feeling any form of pain. It often sees things as being complicated and will often complicate the conflict. It will persist even if doing so may be to our detriment.

By contrast, our True Self wants to experience, connect, create and celebrate. It simplifies. It wants to heal and grow from any conflict and knows that it may have to go through its pain to do so. Finally, our True Self knows that it can co-create its life by connecting to its Higher Power — something impossible for the false self. Learning to differentiate these two is an ongoing process. [109,112,116]

Working through our Core Issues

Our core issues may be about needing to be in control, all-or-none thinking and behaving, fear of abandonment or something else. Whatever it is, working through our core issues is intimately intertwined with nearly every aspect of recovery. Each of us has several or even all of these to work through as we get to know ourself, others and God better and better. I describe these core issues further in Chapters 11 and 12, in Chapter 23 of *A Gift to Myself* and in *Co-dependence*.

Table 15.2. Some Characteristics of the True Self and the False or Co-dependent Self

True Self	False or Co-dependent Self
• Authentic Self	• Unauthentic self, mask
• True Self	• False self, persona
• Genuine	• Ungenuine, "as-if" personality
• Spontaneous	• Plans and plods
• Expansive, loving	• Contracting, fearful
• Giving, communicating	• Withholding
• Accepting of self and others	• Envious, critical, idealized, perfectionistic
• Compassionate	• Other-oriented, overly conforming
• Loves unconditionally	• Loves conditionally
• Feels feelings, including appropriate, spontaneous, current anger	• Denies or hides feelings, including long-held anger (resentment)
• Assertive	• Aggressive and/or passive
• Intuitive	• Rational, logical
• Child Within, Inner Child; ability to be childlike	• Overdeveloped parent/adult scripts; may be childish
• Needs to play and have fun	• Avoids play and fun
• Vulnerable	• Pretends always to be strong
• Powerful in true sense	• Limited power
• Trusting	• Distrusting
• Enjoys being nurtured	• Avoids being nurtured
• Surrenders	• Controls, withdraws
• Self-indulgent	• Self-righteous
• Simplifies	• Complicates; is "rational"
• Wants to be real, connect, experience, create and love	• Wants to be right, control and win. Tells us the *opposite* of what we want and need.
• Nondefensive, though may at times use self ("ego") defenses	• Defensive
• Connected to its Higher Power	• Believes *it* is Higher Power
• Open to the unconscious	• Blocks unconscious material
• Remembers our Oneness	• Forgets our Oneness; feels separate
• Free to grow	• Tends to act out unconscious often painful patterns repeatedly
• Private self	• Public self

Learning that the Core of our Being is Love

This task and the one that follows tend to come into our awareness in the most advanced stage of our recovery (Stage Three). While we can contemplate and even experience these to some degree at any time, they tend to come most easily after we have completed Stage Two recovery.

As we slowly peel away the constricting layers from around our true identity, we become progressively more free. These layers are a combination of the stuff of our false self and our collection of what others have dumped onto us over the years. As we slowly shed these painful layers, we begin to experience the fact that at the core of our being we are a spark of creative, Unconditional Love. All we have ever wanted or needed is to be that Love and extend it to others. I explore this concept and experience in the last chapter.

Becoming a Co-creator

To co-create is to let go of our boundaries and join as our True Self in loving harmony with our Higher Power. By so doing we extend our Love and expand ourself so that, in concert with the God of our understanding, we can co-create success and joy in our life. This appears to be the most evolved experience that we can have as a human being. When we reach this final stage of recovery, we have transformed our co-dependence into co-creation. [112]

We can use the process of co-creation in any of our relationships. Here I do all that I can to resolve and heal any conflicts that I may have in any relationship and then, in the spirit of love, turn the rest over to my Higher Power.

This long process of wounding and recovery can be illustrated in a "U" shaped curve, as shown in Figure 15.6 on the next two pages.

Conclusion

This chapter gives an outline of the stages and process of some of the basic actions I can take to actualize or realize my Real Self. Without being real, it will be hard for me to set healthy boundaries. Learning to set or let go of my boundaries in a healthy way is a slow process that usually takes several years of working a full recovery program in Stage Two recovery. In Stage Three I continue to heal myself and grow. Here I begin to let go of some of my boundaries with my self, close others and my Higher Power, all of which continue to open me to a richer and more enjoyable life.

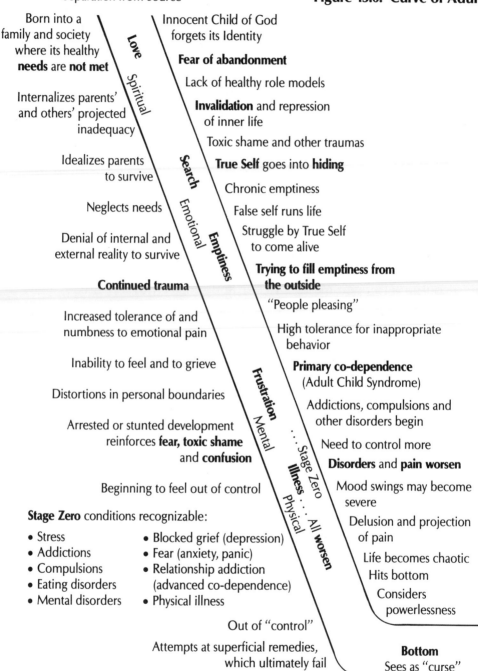

Figure 15.6. Curve of Adult

Separation from Source*

Born into a
family and society
where its healthy
needs are **not met**

Innocent Child of God
forgets its Identity

Fear of abandonment

Lack of healthy role models

Internalizes parents'
and others' projected
inadequacy

Love
Spiritual

Invalidation and repression
of inner life

Toxic shame and other traumas

Idealizes parents
to survive

Search
Emotional

True Self goes into **hiding**

Chronic emptiness

Neglects needs

False self runs life

Denial of internal and
external reality to survive

Emptiness

Struggle by True Self
to come alive

Continued trauma

**Trying to fill emptiness from
the outside**

"People pleasing"

Increased tolerance of and
numbness to emotional pain

High tolerance for inappropriate
behavior

Inability to feel and to grieve

Frustration
Mental

Primary co-dependence
(Adult Child Syndrome)

Distortions in personal boundaries

Addictions, compulsions and
other disorders begin

Arrested or stunted development
reinforces **fear, toxic shame**
and **confusion**

Stage Zero

Need to control more

Disorders and **pain worsen**

Beginning to feel out of control

Illness
Physical

All worsen

Mood swings may become
severe

Stage Zero conditions recognizable:

Delusion and projection
of pain

- Stress
- Addictions
- Compulsions
- Eating disorders
- Mental disorders

- Blocked grief (depression)
- Fear (anxiety, panic)
- Relationship addiction
(advanced co-dependence)
- Physical illness

Life becomes chaotic

Hits bottom

Considers
powerlessness

Out of "control"

Attempts at superficial remedies,
which ultimately fail

Bottom
Sees as "curse"

*Higher Power, God/Goddess/All-That-Is

©Charles L. Whitfield 19

dependence Wounding and Recovery   Co-creation

Selfless service

Emptiness filled most of time   Serenity

Learning power of Unconditional Love   *Love*   Learning Core
of Being is Love

Spirituality and serenity deepen

Remembers Identity

Recycling and handling little "relapses"   *Spiritual*   Learning God's Will

Beginning, continuing or deepening   *Experientially*
of **spiritual practices**   knows God

Possible inability to relate   *Stage Three*   → Coping. Growth
experientially to God   stops about here

Learning difference between   Learning to like self
necessary and unnecessary pain   **Emptiness lessens**

Able to set healthy boundaries   Realizes *Child Within*
and limits   *experientially*

Experientially learning and knowing
the difference between True Self   *Self Discovery*   Learning about age regression
and false self   **Grieving**

Working through **core issues**   *Emotional*   Lessening tolerance for
inappropriate behavior

Learning to tolerate emotional pain   *Stage Two*

Learning **needs**   Learning to grieve

Learning healthy **boundaries**   Discovers Child Within *cognitively*

Learning to recognize feelings   *and continues*   Looks progressively deeper
into inner life

Begins Stage Two full recovery   *Mental*   Seeks solution outside of false self

Awakens to **adult child** issues   Wonders if there is more

Unaware of or denies   → Coping. Growth stops about here
adult child issues   Frustration with results
of Stage One recovery

Relationship
difficulties with   Other addictions and compulsions
self, others and God   surface

Considers needs — physical, mental,

Frustration with   *Stage One*   emotional, spiritual
repeated crises   *Recovery Begins*   Begins learning inner life of True Self

Hope increases   *Physical*   Pain and disorders decrease

Toxicity lessens   **Begins Stage One** Full Recovery Program

Asks for help   **Seeks solution outside of false self**

Admits powerlessness

nsiders pain   → Limited or no recovery
opportunity   Cancer, cardiovascular or other
debilitating physical or mental disease

16

"No" Is A Complete Sentence – Other Principles Of Boundaries And Limits

Throughout this book I have suggested ways to recognize boundary problems and to set healthy boundaries and limits, while integrating these within a healthy self in relationships and during the process of recovery. In this chapter I describe some additional aspects of boundaries and relationships.

Being Assertive

Being assertive is a healthy and effective way of expressing and setting boundaries. When I am *assertive*, I get my wants and needs met without attacking or purposefully hurting another.[100a] By contrast, when I am *aggressive* with another person, I usually hurt them and often create a conflict that may be hard to resolve. It is often a lose-lose situation, in contrast to a win-win one if I am assertive. A way to measure whether I have been assertive is to check out how both of us are feeling right now in the relationship about the encounter. If we both feel good about it, the chances are that I was assertive. But if either of us is feeling bad, then it is possible that one or both of us was aggressive. And it is also likely that the conflict is unresolved.

In being *assertive* I am usually setting a *healthy boundary* or limit — either directly or associated with whatever it is that I am asserting myself about. For example, you may want to go to a particular movie of your choice, and you ask me to go with you. If I am not interested in seeing that movie, I can be assertive and simply say in a calm voice, "No" or "No, thank you." In this particular case I have expressed my wants and have thereby also set a boundary in a healthy way. I have not raised my voice or yelled at you, and I have not attacked you in any other way. It is now up to you to decide further about your wish to see the movie.

By saying "No," I have expressed myself, my own wants and needs. That simple expression is usually adequate. In this sense, "No" is a complete sentence, and I don't need to say anything more or give a reason why I said no. A problem can develop when a perhaps still-wounded person believes they have to give a reason or explanation for saying no. This kind of behavior can end up complicating and confusing the simple clarity of the appropriately expressed "No." If I elaborate in this way, I may start to get defensive and we may even get into an unnecessary argument.

To learn to be assertive takes practice in a *safe environment over time,* ideally in the context of a full recovery program. This is because I cannot learn to be assertive and thereby set healthy boundaries without having a healthy self from which to *be* assertive, as illustrated in Figure 4.3.

Teachers and Assistants

Throughout our lives we are continually learning about boundaries in all kinds of ways and from all kinds of people, places and things. We learn about them from such people as our parents and other family members, teachers, peers and elsewhere, including therapists and counselors.

In any of these relationships where there is a substantial power difference — which is usually the case in all of the above except peer relationships — there may be special rules that are different from those usually found among peers. Some of these rules may include that while there may be a feeling of friendship at times, a traditional friendship is not the goal in this particular relationship. Nor is pleasing the other or getting them to like you or love you. Rather, for parents the goal may be healthy parenting, or in the workplace getting the job done, or with education learning how to learn. Yet in each of these there is always a chance for closeness and intimacy. Such closeness and intimacy may not be appropriate with work colleagues or bosses, but may be with family, best friends or lovers. With school teachers it is somewhere in between.

Therapists and Counselors

With therapists and counselors it is even more appropriate to let down our usual boundaries and gradually tell our truth. While we cannot expect them to "fix" us or have "magical powers" over us, we can expect several things from them regarding boundaries. The first is that the therapist or counselor will in their own way *model* having healthy boundaries, such as starting and ending the therapy session on time and not taking phone calls or other interruptions during the session. They will also remain respectful and non-invasive of certain of our boundaries. For others, as they help us probe the nooks and crannies of our experience and truth, invading some of our boundaries may be appropriate and even desirable. This may also include pointing out our unhealthy boundaries whenever they occur (Table 16.1).

Table 16.1. Therapists' Assisting in Healthy Boundary Formation

1. Model healthy boundaries
2. Remain respectful and noninvasive of their boundaries
3. Point out unhealthy boundaries
4. Help with increasing awareness and use of inner life (i.e., healing their Real Self)
5. Help discover, reclaim and maintain healthy boundaries

Examples of Pointing out Unhealthy Boundaries in Family Therapy

In family and couples therapy, there are indicators of boundary invasions and distortion, such as who interrupts or completes information for others, who supplies information and who gives help. Looking for affiliations, coalitions, overinvolved dyads (twosomes) or triangles and other patterns is also helpful in assessing boundaries in families and couples. In working with subsystems, such as parents, Minuchin says, "Boundaries between subsystems are also necessary, and if parents intrude in sibling conflicts, or adolescents disqualify parents or intrude into the spouses' area, or grandparents join with grandchildren against their parents, or spouses bring their parents into coalition against their spouses, the therapist has available a variety of boundary making techniques. Sometimes the therapist introduces a rule at the beginning of therapy. He may say: 'In this room, I have only one rule. It is a small rule, but apparently very difficult for this family to follow. It is that no person should talk for another person, or tell another person how this person feels or thinks. People should tell their own story and own their own memory.' Variations on this rule allow the therapist to enforce boundaries and to punctuate family members' intrusion into other members' psychological space as 'disobedience to the rule.' Intrusions, affiliations, or coalitions can be blocked [framed] as talking for another person, or imagining that person's thoughts and future actions."[79]

My Inner Life

Crucial in this entire process is helping us to achieve an increasing awareness and use of the inner life of our Real Self (see Figure 1.3). This is the key to healthy boundary formation — self-realization, self-actualization and self-knowledge — as we live from and as our true identity, who we really are. In general, the therapist or counselor can assist us in discovering, reclaiming and maintaining healthy boundaries in whichever stage of recovery we might currently be.

My Recovery Plan

A way that I can use the therapist's expertise in all of the above is to enlist their assistance in my making a personal recovery plan for myself. I describe this process in *A Gift to Myself, Co-dependence* and the booklet "My Recovery Plan — for Stage Two." That recovery plan is *itself* a kind of healthy boundary, in that it is a declaration of what I want to happen for me. Boundaries may also be a *part* of the plan itself: e.g., listing "unhealthy boundaries" or "boundary problems" as one of my problems that I want to work on, as shown below.

Table 16.2 My Recovery Plan		
Problem	**What I want to happen**	**How I plan to accomplish that**
Unhealthy boundaries	Have healthy boundaries in my life	Group Therapy adult-child focused, weekly, long-term
		Twelve-Step Fellowship attendance weekly
		Keep a journal

These are but examples. I can write these in any way that I want and need to assist me in working on having healthy boundaries.

For further principles on boundaries and limits for therapists and counselors in the therapeutic relationship, I have written a booklet, "Boundaries in Counseling and Therapy." It is available from Health Communications. Also, Marilyn Peterson has written *At Personal Risk: Boundary Violations in Professional-Client Relationships,* published by W.W. Norton.

Boundaries and Certain *Stage Zero* Disorders

Stage Zero disorders are those listed in the current diagnostic code books of psychological and physical disorders. It is in a Stage One full recovery program where a person can address, stabilize or heal that disorder (see Table 15.1). While there are no hard and fast rules about these disorders, perhaps among the most affected by boundary distortions, violations and problems are most of the psychoses, several personality disorders, active addictions and post-traumatic stress disorder (PTSD).

Thought Disorder

Having a "thought disorder," psychotic persons are unable to set healthy boundaries with much of their inner life, including their intrusive thoughts.[12,29a,38,91] These may be aggravated by voices that they hear from within themself — some of which we might otherwise call old "tapes" or negative messages that we learned as we got wounded by our dysfunctional family and society of origin. While taking antipsychotic drugs may help decrease these voices and the other symptoms of active psychosis, many people with this disorder who stabilize appropriately can eventually go on to a Stage Two full recovery program and heal in a deeper way.

Personality Disorders

While all of the personality disorders display unhealthy boundaries, two of them do so in an exaggerated way: borderline personality disorder and narcissistic personality disorder. The borderline person often lets in and projects toxic material to the outside world, while the narcissistic tends mostly to project.* People with paranoid personality disorder may do the same, but their focus is more obsessing on ex-

---

* The person with antisocial personality disorder also projects in a similar way as the narcissist, and has a similar or worse prognosis with therapy.

aggerated stories of what the world is doing to them. While many people with mild to moderately severe borderline personality disorder can make a fair to excellent recovery if they work long and hard in a Stage Two full recovery program, few with narcissistic personality disorder tend to be able to do so. Like borderlines, those with other personality disorders can also recover in varying degrees, but their time required for recovery usually exceeds five years.

Addictions

Active addiction that is uncomplicated by any of the above disorders displays numerous boundary distortions. Their earliest recovery in a Stage One program includes their personally setting healthy boundaries against using their drug, substance or behavior of choice, as well as against other people and places where they might be at a high risk of using again. Another healthy boundary that is useful in all of the Stage Zero disorders is to let go of unhealthy boundaries or walls against safe others and, if they choose, their Higher Power, and let them in — asking for and accepting help. Most people with otherwise uncomplicated addiction can later reach a successful recovery as an adult child in a Stage Two full recovery program, and the same is true for those with PTSD.

Post-Traumatic Stress Disorder

In post-traumatic stress disorder (PTSD) the person, wounded by substantial past traumatic experiences, unconsciously allows a disabling stress reaction to be triggered in their present life by anything that may remind them of those past traumas. People with uncomplicated PTSD can usually enter immediately into a Stage Two full recovery program and improve over time.

The diagnosis or self-recognition of the *adult child* syndrome, a major manifestation of which is the condition called *co-dependence*, pervades all of the recovery Stages, from

Zero to Two. If uncomplicated by any of the above active disorders or similar ones, it generally has a good prognosis in a Stage Two full recovery program. These two conditions, which are essentially the same, while not being the *cause* of any specific Stage Zero disorders, can *underlie* and *aggravate* any of them. While the principles about boundaries discussed throughout this book may be used at any time, they are generally most effectively addressed and healed in Stage Two recovery.

Repairing and Building Boundaries

To repair and build boundaries, I can follow many of the principles described throughout this book. While I know of no shortcuts, a summary of the process follows. I heal my True Self, and to do that I need to go within, into my inner life. Over time I . . .

- Identify and grieve my ungrieved hurts, losses and traumas
- Get my healthy human needs met
- Work through my core recovery issues

I begin to identify how I was mistreated in my childhood — my hurts, losses and traumas — and I grieve them over time. I identify how my boundaries were violated and learn to prevent these kinds of violations in the future. I have briefly described this entire healing process in the previous chapter, and in more detail in *A Gift To Myself* and *Co-dependence: Healing the Human Condition*.

I can also examine the state of my boundaries in my *present relationships*, including my family, and begin to clean them up. As I become progressively more aware of my True Self, I will likely realize more and more ways that my boundaries were violated as a child — and as an adult. As I heal from these violations, I will generate healthy boundaries both inside and outside of me, including in my present relationships. [52]

This process of setting boundaries is not easy, and many people close to us may try to sabotage our healing. Lerner says, "Do not expect others to automatically appreciate the effort it takes to establish clear boundaries. On the contrary, those close to us may become upset that we're forming a separate identity. Be assured, however, that as our physical, emotional, intellectual and spiritual realities become clear and strong, relationships will become healthier and more satisfying. In the end it is up to us to form our boundaries with others. No one can do this for us. Repairing damaged boundaries may require the guidance of a mentor, sponsor or a therapist, but the responsibility for our healing lies with us."[59]

A Personal Bill of Rights

As part of my healing I can begin to discover that I have rights as an individual human being. As children and even as adults, we may have been treated by others as though we had few or no rights. We may have ourselves come to believe that we had no rights. And we may be living our lives now as though we have none.

As we recover and heal our True Self, we can put together our personal "bill of rights." As part of the therapy groups that I have facilitated, I have asked the group members to consider what rights they have, to write them out and to share them with the group. The following is a compilation of rights that several groups have created.

1. I have numerous choices in my life beyond mere survival.
2. I have the right to discover and know my Child Within.
3. I have the right to grieve over what I didn't get that I needed or what I got that I didn't need or want.
4. I have the right to follow my own values and standards.

5. I have the right to recognize and accept my own value system as appropriate.
6. I have the right to say no to anything when I feel I am not ready, it is unsafe or it violates my values.
7. I have the right to dignity and respect.
8. I have the right to make decisions.
9. I have the right to determine and honor my own priorities.
10. I have the right to have my needs and wants respected by others.
11. I have the right to terminate conversations with people who make me feel put down and humiliated.
12. I have the right not to be responsible for others' behavior, actions, feelings or problems.
13. I have the right to make mistakes and not have to be perfect.
14. I have the right to expect honesty from others.
15. I have the right to all of my feelings.
16. I have the right to be angry at someone I love.
17. I have the right to be uniquely me, without feeling that I'm not good enough.
18. I have the right to feel scared and to say, "I'm afraid."
19. I have the right to experience and then let go of fear, guilt and shame.
20. I have the right to make decisions based on my feelings, my judgment or any reason that I choose.
21. I have the right to change my mind at any time.
22. I have the right to be happy.
23. I have the right to stability, i.e., "roots" and stable healthy relationships of my choice.
24. I have the right to my own personal space and time needs.
25. I have the right to be relaxed, playful and frivolous.
26. I have the right to be flexible and be comfortable with doing so.
27. I have the right to change and grow.

28. I have the right to be open to improve my communication skills so that I may be understood.
29. I have the right to make friends and be comfortable around people.
30. I have the right to be in a nonabusive environment.
31. I have the right to be healthier than those around me.
32. I have the right to take care of myself, no matter what.
33. I have the right to grieve over actual or threatened losses.
34. I have the right to trust others who earn my trust.
35. I have the right to forgive others and to forgive myself.
36. I have the right to give and to receive unconditional love.

You may wish to consider whether you have any of these rights. My belief is that every human being has every one of these rights and more. Healthy boundaries can help us formulate our rights, and in a reciprocal fashion, knowing that we have these rights can strengthen our boundaries.

17
---•---

Spirituality – Letting Go
Of Boundaries And Limits

So far I have talked mostly about some important components and dynamics in relationships and how *setting* healthy boundaries relates to them. Now I will look more at how to *let go* of boundaries and limits. This is because before I can let go of many things, I have to know experientially *exactly what it is* that I am letting go of. The possibilities here comprise most of the material and dynamics in my inner life, including my boundaries and limits. And this is why I place this chapter at the end of this book — because before I can successfully let go of a boundary, I have to know exactly what it is.

My briefest definition of spirituality is that it is about our relationships with our self, others and the Universe or God/Goddess/All-That-Is. It is not about religion. While religion may relate to it, spirituality at the same time transcends it. While we have a relationship with our self, others, and if we choose, our Higher Power, we commonly involve *each* of these three basic relationships whenever we are involved with *any* person, place or thing.

The Journey

While our journey here on Earth — and beyond — is a Divine Mystery, we can consider how we and our boundaries may relate to the spiritual. Perhaps in another time and another place, we were a part of our Higher Power, which itself is boundaryless. And for some reason, as spiritual beings we temporarily left our Higher Power to have a human experience, as I illustrate in Figure 17.1. But as part of the Plan or Mystery, we had to *forget* most of what we knew or had experienced before we came to live here on Earth so that we might live out the Mystery more efficiently.

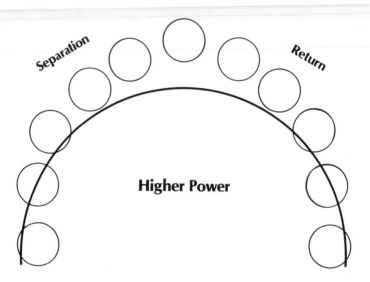

Initiation

Separation

Return

Higher Power

Figure 17.1. A Concept of the Evolution of Human Boundary and Higher Power. The Journey from Separation to Return.

So as a newly born and now separate being, I went through the adventure of first thinking I was fused with my family of origin, and then was wounded in some degree by them and by my society of origin. This left me feeling empty and alone. Because the pain was too great for my vulnerable True Self (Child Within) to bear, my Real Self went into hiding, as I describe on page 57. Since the resulting emptiness ached and hurt so much, I tried to fill it with people, places, things and behaviors from outside of me — anything to lessen the pain. But I eventually became frustrated, because none of those things seemed to work in filling my emptiness for very long.

Utterly frustrated, perhaps even hitting one or more "bottoms," I eventually let down some of my walls and opened myself to the possibility that I needed to look at myself and the world in a different way. So I went within and began to discover my Real Self and its experiential connection to the God of my understanding.

But to expose that, my vulnerable self, to a sometimes mistreating world, I had to learn to set healthy boundaries. These boundaries then helped me to maintain the integrity and well-being of the real me. Little by little, I began to realize my True Self in progressive increments, and setting boundaries worked for me.

Letting Go

I also learned that setting boundaries and limits didn't always work — that there were times when I could also *let go* of them to help me get what I wanted and needed. This process is illustrated in the following story:

> There was a farmer who had a strong, comfortable house and a lot of fields. He kept all of the birds and creatures away from his crops with traps and fences. One day he stood in the middle of his fields to welcome the animals. He stayed there from dawn till dusk, with his arms outstretched. But not a single animal came, not a creature appeared. They were terrified of his traps and fences.

Healthy boundaries are *flexible* (see page 115), and work best according to my wants and needs at the time. There are numerous times throughout my day that I can open up to people, places and things and let them in. During my recovery I have also learned to differentiate those who may be safe from those who are not safe (Table 8.2).

There are countless ways to open myself up to the world and to the Universe — to my self, others and God. Some of these may include my being real, being aware of my inner life, reading spiritual literature, meditating and praying. In doing any of these and more, I let go of my boundaries and I drop down my walls.

Evolution of Our *Self-Boundaries* and God

As described above under "The Journey," as we live out the Divine Mystery, we are first a part of God/Goddess/All-That-Is. Then we separate from God, come to live on this Earth and undergo an initiation — a series of learning experiences. And then, perhaps richer for the experience, we gradually return to God (Figure 17.1). Looking back, we may see that while we *appeared* to separate from God, *we never really did. A Course in Miracles* describes this experience as "the separation that never was."[25] The Perennial Philosophy — the experiential, spiritual and religious wisdom over the ages — agrees.[48a,119]

In our search for self and God, most of us need to use spiritual practices to realize these two aspects of ourselves — our selfhood, with boundaries, and our boundarylessness. And the paradox is that each move that we make toward that boundarylessness, toward Unity consciousness with All-That-Is, can push us further away from It. This is because there is no *path* to serenity, to the core of our being, which is Love. There is no way to arrive at that which already and always *is*. In his book *No Boundary*, Wilber said, "Unity consciousness is not so much a particular wave as it is the *water* itself. . . . as long as you are wave-jumping in search of wetness, you obviously will never discover that wetness exists in its purity on whatever wave you're riding now. Unity consciousness . . . is every wave of present experience just as it is." God is boundaryless, and we are each a crucial part of that One.[25,119]

The Frustration Begins

But we get frustrated because it can be hard to let go of our boundaries and surrender into the experience of our life and into the Mystery — with the God of our understanding. There may be at least three reasons for this difficulty. First, I may not have healed my True Self by a process similar to Stage Two recovery. I may not know, realize and be able to live from and as my True Self. If I can't, it is unlikely that I can experientially know God, because my True Self is the only part of my psychological apparatus that *can* know God. The false self can't, and as long as I try to live from it, I will feel empty. This is why Stage Two recovery is so important. It is where I learn to set healthy boundaries and limits — as well as to let go of them whenever it is appropriate to my healthy wants and needs.

Not Knowing How to Let Go

The second reason is that I may not know *how* to surrender and know God. This is what spiritual practices can do — they can help me in my learning to let go. Regular meditation, prayer, reading spiritual literature, attending a Twelve-Step meeting or a religious service that actually nourishes me, or some other spiritual practice — these can assist me in my opening to safe others and to the God of my understanding.

The third reason is related to the first two. It is related to the frustration that I may feel when these above two processes don't seem to work for me. And this reason may be due to another paradox. From the teachings of the spiritual masters and numerous holy books, the message is the same: that we have it, Unity consciousness, Serenity, *now*.[25,110,111]

But we forget, and we sometimes resist. And so we both seek and resist Unity consciousness in a circular fashion, through a cycle of involution and evolution, by self-contraction and self-expansion, by setting boundaries and letting go of them. And it is this circle on which we seem to be constantly moving. The circle is the ancient Chinese and Zen symbol for perfection, which it encloses in the Yin-Yang symbol.

It may be that each spiritual practice both frustrates us and shows us a type of our resistance. Experientially understanding such a concept can give us a glimpse of Unity consciousness because that which *sees* the frustration and the resistance is free of them.[119] We can then be free to look upon all of our experience as a whole, as it is now, and to see and experience that both the seeking and resisting are part of the experience of the True Self as it climbs all over and explores the Mystery — until it finally surrenders and becomes a part of it.

Hitting a Psycho-Spiritual Bottom

But I may encounter another frustration from the next insight: Everything I *do,* including seeking inner peace through spiritual practice, can *itself* be a kind of resistance as long as I see myself as separate from others and God. At this point, all may seem lost, and I may even feel a "dark night of the soul." Everything seems wrong because it is as though every *move* that I make, every *action* that I take is also a movement *away* from Serenity. Utterly frustrated, I may here hit a kind of psycho-spiritual "bottom" and thereby become open and vulnerable in a healthy way — open to just giving up the search, and just experiencing and *being,* with no boundaries. It is here that the entire movement and process of our frustration, resistance and emptiness winds down, and we see that we *are* Unity consciousness, we are already and always an inherent and important part of God. We are One. There are no boundaries, and we are not separate.[119] Boundaries are no longer useful.

Final Letting Go

Wilber said, "It thus becomes apparent why the search for Unity consciousness was so exasperating. Everything we tried to do was wrong because everything was already and eternally right. Even what appeared as primal resistance to Brahman [i.e., Unity consciousness, Oneness with God] was actually a movement of Brahman because there is *nothing but* Brahman [God]. There never was, nor will there ever be, anytime other than Now. What appeared as that primal moving *away* from Now [also God] was really an original movement *of* Now. . . . the ocean waves surge freely against the shore, wetting the pebbles and shells."[119]

The search, the woundedness, the addictions and compulsions and other "diseases," the struggle, the frustration and the growth of our recovery and our life are all a part of our experience as we live out this part of the Divine Mystery. When we move away from God, we hurt and when we let go *into* God, we feel love and peace. As we more authentically know and trust our self and God, so can we know safe others more intimately in our life. In our close and intimate relationships with them, we can also let go of any boundaries as appropriate, which may then nourish our relationship.

Good Fences?

In his poem "Mending Wall" (reproduced here in its entirety), Robert Frost expresses some of his personal experiences with boundaries.[36]

Mending Wall

Something there is that doesn't love a wall,
That sends the frozen-ground-swell under it,
And spills the upper bowlders in the sun;
And makes gaps even two can pass abreast.
The work of hunters is another thing:
I have come after them and made repair
Where they have left not one stone on a stone,
But they would have the rabbit out of hiding,

To please the yelping dogs. The gaps I mean,
No one has seen them made or heard them made,
But at spring mending-time we find them there.
I let my neighbor know beyond the hill;
And on a day we meet to walk the line
And set the wall between us once again.
We keep the wall between us as we go.
To each the bowlders that have fallen to each.
And some are loaves and some so nearly balls
We have to use a spell to make them balance:
"Stay where you are until our backs are turned!"

We wear our fingers rough with handling them.
Oh, just another kind of outdoor game,
One on a side. It comes to little more.
There where it is we do not need the wall:
He is all pine and I am apple-orchard.
My apple trees will never get across
And eat the cones under his pines, I tell him.
He only says, "Good fences make good neighbors."
Spring is the mischief in me, and I wonder
If I could put a notion in his head:
"Why do they make good neighbors? Isn't it
Where there are cows? But here there are no cows.
Before I built a wall I'd ask to know
What I was walling in or walling out,
And to whom I was like to give offense.
Something there is that doesn't love a wall,
That wants it down!" I could say "Elves" to him,
But it's not elves exactly, and I'd rather
He said it for himself. I see him there,
Bringing a stone grasped firmly by the top
In each hand, like an old-stone savage armed.
He moves in darkness, as it seems to me,
Not of woods only and the shade of trees.
He will not go behind his father's saying,
And he likes having thought of it so well
He says again, "Good fences make good neighbors."

My sense is that the writer is having an internal debate between three parts of himself: his false self which makes walls, his True Self which sets healthy boundaries, and his Higher Self which helps let go of them. The "Something there is that doesn't love a wall" and the "work of hunters" are aspects of the creative unconscious that are forever toppling the stones as boundaries. While at times, "Good fences [do] make good neighbors," i.e., healthy boundaries can be useful, there are also times where boundaries are *not* necessary. "There where it is we do not need the wall: He is all pine and I am apple orchard."

Perhaps his most important statement is, "Before I built a wall I'd ask to know/What I was walling in or walling out." To me this expresses the importance of being aware of my inner life as a guide to set the boundary. And near the end, "He moves in darkness" shows the opposite: the unconscious of the false self, building a wall. Only two lines are repeated: "Good fences make good neighbors" and "Something there is that doesn't love a wall." These emphasize the two sides of the coin: setting healthy boundaries when appropriate, and also letting go when that may be useful.

Humility

Being humble is neither groveling nor being a doormat. It is instead being open to experiencing and learning about self, others and God. In this sense, having humility involves letting go of our boundaries.

Gaining humility is a major milestone in recovery and life. It usually signifies a life transformation, in that the person flows more with life, functions better and tends to experience more fulfilling relationships.[110]

The Between

For millennia spirituality and religion, while related, have been differentiated by religion's outer focus on the "there and then," a God that is "out there" beyond human existence, and this has frustrated many spiritual seekers. Yearning for direct experience of God, the spiritual or mystical path goes within, in search of self and God. While these two may exist comfortably at times, they usually co-exist in an uneasy alliance, and history has been a blood-stained chronicle of formal believers persecuting and exterminating mystics, non-believers and other faiths because of their differences.[9]

Drawing on the work of theologian Martin Buber, Berenson suggests a third approach to realizing the spiritual and God: "the between," in which one sees divinity as inherent in the *connections* of our *relationships*, in the psycho-spiritual space between. Buber says, "On the far side of the subjective, on this side of the objective, on the narrow ridge, where *I* and *Thou* meet, there is the realm of 'between.' This reality, whose disclosure has begun in our time, shows the way, leading beyond individualism and collectivism, for the life decision of future generations. Here the genuine third alternative is indicated, the knowledge of which will help bring about the genuine person again and to establish genuine community."[8,9,17,18]

After we have healed in Stage Two recovery, this idea of "the between" helps us open our boundaries and let others and God into our experience. Berenson says, "We arrive at a new, systemic conception and perception of God, which again can only be expressed paradoxically: God is immanent within I-Thou relationships; yet entering into dialogue or relation also can provide a sense of a transcendent, absolute presence. To be completely relating in the here and now brings forth a sense of the Beyond, and being aware of the reality of the Beyond bring some into more intimate relation with others. This relationship with God does not remove one from the world but brings one into more immediate contact and connection."[8]

Bonding

If we remove the "u" from the *bound* of boundary, it becomes *bond*. To bond is to join with or become one. We let go into the other. We drop the two separate "you's."

Having been abused or mistreated in some way, adult children of dysfunctional families don't usually get to bond with their parents. Try as they may, they don't feel safe enough to let go and trust them completely. But they may have someone, somewhere during their life, with whom they feel some closeness, and at times they may feel a sort of bond with them. In recovery they require the sense of feeling safe before they can let go with someone and be real.

As we recover, we can begin to bond in some way with safe others. Eventually we may be able to trust enough to *let go* into an intimate relationship, as I described on page 130. Some intimate relationships can be open enough to bond even deeper. Harris said, "When two people bond spiritually their hearts are open to each other without a separate sense of themselves as an individual. The two are one new entity. As though they are in a lover's embrace — heart to heart — the energy that flows between them joins them in one heartbeat."[43,44]

But even in a healthy, intimate relationship there is space to breathe (Figure 17.2). There are usually times when the two are bonded, united and intimate — but *not* fused or enmeshed. Then there are times when they are close. And there are times when they are physically and psychologically separate.

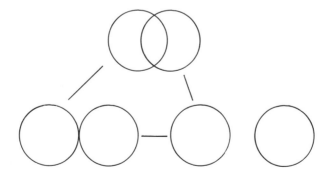

Figure 17.2. The Flow of an Intimate Relationship

Each of these is needed to keep balance and flow in the relationship, so that each can live as a whole, separate and unique individual — together. Healthy boundaries — and boundarylessness.

Appendix

—— • ——

Boundaries, Energy And The Body

by Barbara Harris*
(author of *Full Circle* and *Spiritual Awakenings*)

From a physical, psychological and spiritual perspective, boundaries can have components of energy. This energy may be derived from the individual boundary setter's inner life and projected or extended outward throughout their day-to-day life. At times this and other forms of energy may be recognized and experienced by others, for example, when one person can read another person's "aura" or energy field.

This energy may be associated with what is called a higher sense perception of psychic energy, wherein a person may have or develop certain psychic abilities, such as somehow knowing what is about to happen. People who have been abused as children and many who have had spiritual awakenings may develop these kinds of higher sense perceptions or "psychic abilities" more often and to a greater degree than the general population.

---

*Charles Whitfield assisted with the writing and editing of this chapter, which is excerpted from Barbara Harris' book *Spiritual Awakenings*.[43]

Kenneth Ring said that ancient spiritual psychological literature links psychic phenomena to the unfolding of a higher form of consciousness. But there is a warning which usually follows about becoming attached to any associated psychic phenomena. From the Buddhist perspective, the attainment of such "powers" is only a minor advantage, and it is of no value in itself for progress toward liberation or serenity. In one who has not yet attained such a state, these psychic abilities are even an impediment, for they may endanger our psycho-spiritual progress by enhancing and strengthening our attachment to our false self (Ring 1984, quote from Golman).

We can be grateful for our psychic awareness and abilities because these higher sense perceptions serve as a reminder that we are connected — that our subtle energy fields overlap and act upon one another, sometimes even at great distances.

Pitfalls

As the masters of ancient spiritual psychologies warned, focusing only on this "talent" (that everyone has, but may not be awake to yet) will create attachments that distract us. Our observations are that many people get caught in this trap and then after a while move on. It seems to be so provocative that it becomes a kind of stopping off point. Then after a while, the person puts their psychic "stuff" away by incorporating it into normal reality. As our transformational journey continues, we realize that these higher sense perceptions are helpful when used with humility and in the act of service.

Even without having been abused as children or experiencing a spiritual awakening, when we heal our True Self on a deeper level some of our higher sense perceptions will emerge. Psychic abilities are our birthright as human beings. With a spiritual awakening, such awareness often becomes obvious quickly instead of emerging gradually. However, it could also overpower us because as unhealed adult children our boundaries are not yet healthy and well defined. With a history of traumatic and abusive childhoods, by lessening our development of healthy boundaries and having a sudden increase in psychic sensitivity, we're likely to pick up others' moods and feelings even more intensely than before any spiritual awakening.

Spiritual Teachers

Another possible pitfall is trying to hurry psychic development by taking lessons or classes from a teacher we may know little about. Before doing so, we suggest reading books from authors who are respected in the field, who show *humility* and *integrity* in their life's work and private life. Next, we suggest that it would be helpful to learn meditation. It is a good way to become more aware of this level of reality. By practicing meditation, we become fine tuned to the subtle levels of our inner life. Then when we know our inner life well, by centering and focusing, we can go behind it, or quiet it down and sense these psychic perceptions.

Neighborhood or community classes on psychic abilities need to be screened carefully, and even then, you can use your gut feelings. If you feel uncomfortable or even faintly afraid, then something is probably not right with what you have chosen. "Psychic teachers" can carry contagious emotional and psychological pathology. That may sound far out, but it is true. Any emotional or mental pathology that they are carrying — even unconscious material — can be projected onto you, through your perhaps vulnerable boundaries, with the psychic "gifts" that you may develop.

Some people explore the psychic realms for ego enhancement rather than for spirituality and self-transformation. Psychic gifts can be big temptations for power seekers. As is shown in the *Sorcerer's Apprentice*, as animated in Disney's "Fantasia," these power junkies may soon learn in dramatic ways what the limits of power are. This is something to be aware of. If you feel it happening to you, you can work

through this stage by surrounding yourself with self-actualized people who show humility and integrity.

Learning Experiences

If you want to take a class in any of these areas, find out
what is being offered at your local community college or
public school's adult education evening program. Check with
others who have already taken the class.

The most rewarding classes I have taken have been on
"healing techniques" from nurses or well-known healers such
as Delores Krieger, Ph.D. and Dora Kunz. They developed
"Therapeutic Touch," a master's degree program for nurses
at New York University. I have taken two of their workshops.
At the first one ten years ago, Dr. Krieger taught us how to
"center." She said that 4,000 nurses had already taken her
course and all but one could do this. The recent figures show
that 40,000 nurses have taken the course and are practicing
Therapeutic Touch in hospitals all over North America. The
few nurses who have been unsuccessful at learning it were
not able to develop the technique of "Centering."

Centering

"Centering" is a focusing within. I ask for God's help and
visualize white light coming in and flowing through my
heart. This is where compassion radiates from, and at that
point I feel it for my client. My intention then is to extend
love and to help the client by relaxing my conscious mind
and observing the universal energies flowing through me
and then into the client. This healing energy has its own
wisdom to balance and make whole. I believe that this centering and extending process is the key to using any type of
psychic ability. We relax and center, turning off the part of
our mind that communicates in words so that a deeper,
more primal and basic sense can be observed.

This centering process is probably more a function of the
right hemisphere of the brain. After a spiritual awakening,

our right hemisphere traits tend to become more active, and centering and meditation will usually come more easily. While we are in that state we are nonlogical, nonlinear and beyond the normal concept of time. Through meditation or any process of quieting ourself, we can still the language-dominated left hemisphere. The problem here is that the more I describe this process to you with words, the farther away we may get from the experience of centering.

Centering involves no words. When my left hemisphere tries to get in and judge or chatter, I see myself in my mind's eye as a camera in the act of recording the scene by seeing and feeling my inner life. I will then be able to recognize any "psychic" information surfacing from my inner life. What I am centering into is the actual experience of my True Self. While extending such a healing,* after 15 or 20 minutes the chatter will start again, and behind it will be an urge to say thank you to the Universe. If done in the spirit of compassion, healing evokes a sense of humility. After I say a prayer of thanks silently, I leave the room. I shake my hands and then run them under cold water to "break the connection" and reactivate my own healthy boundaries.

Defining Psychic Abilities

A person who can perceive multidimensional aspects of reality is psychic. In our ordinary state of consciousness, our mind takes in vast amounts of information — just as you are reading this information right now. Our brain is in constant motion, negotiating our focus and screening out the excess. While doing so is essential for conducting our normal affairs, it can upstage our True Self — which is already and inherently psychic. The True Self has access to a wider range of incoming information, some of which is subtle. The ability to sense in these deeper ways through

---

*I prefer to call it a "Helping." My role is as a helper. The actual healing is co- created between the client and the God of their understanding.

centering in the True Self is natural. This knowledge can communicate through symbols, as in dreams or waking visions (flashes of a scene that are so fast that they register as a sudden memory more than a vision), and in numerous other ways.

This knowledge also communicates through our experience of a direct, intuitive knowing. I may sometimes perceive it through a felt sense, and sometimes it is just there within me. When I am in this state, my information does not come from feeling the other person. I recognize this information within me — within my own inner life — and I can *recognize it as not my own*. Occasionally, *deja vu* comes into what would otherwise be an ordinary scene. I feel as if I have done this before. What I call "future memories" register in the same way as *deja vu* does, but I have a felt sense that this is part of the future.

I can sometimes even see this multidimensional reality. There are fields — emotional, mental, spiritual, etc. — surrounding a physical form. As in an *aura*, these fields are made of radiant energies that have varying degrees of color and surround us like a giant semi-transparent egg. Our fields may interact with other people's fields, giving us information about the other. There are many people today operating in high positions who have these abilities, and this is one reason why they are successful. Whether they work in politics, education, corporations, science, the creative arts or elsewhere, part of what we have called "creativity" and "genius" comes from some of these abilities. But few of these gifted people talk about their higher abilities. They just do their work, and they usually do it well.

Psychic Abilities and Relationships

We may first become aware of this multidimensional reality or "felt sense" in a close loving relationship. When I teach at universities, a student or two will raise their hands and smile as they tell me of having this special connection with their boyfriend or girlfriend — at times knowing the phone is going to ring, knowing when the other is unhappy or hurt, etc. They tell me that what the other person feels, they too feel, whether it is joyful or painful. I suggest that they stay with the subtlety of the feeling. We can do so by tuning out the outer mind and focusing on the vague feeling of direct or intuitive "knowing," a process called "centering." They can have direct access to their subconscious mind and even beyond to the transpersonal or superconscious mind. By being open to our inner life and ignoring the usual noise and preconceived ideas of the outer world, we are free to explore the multilevel aspects of our reality. This is a kind of fine tuning of our inner life, which can allow us to perceive these fields.

In *Full Circle* I told the story of an experience I had — picking up my mother's feelings 1700 miles away when she was in a hospital. I felt a pain in my upper leg at the same time that she was having a bone marrow biopsy. My leg gave way from the shock of the pain, and I fell. I had no knowledge beforehand of her having a painful procedure. When I talked with her on the phone the next day and she told me, I realized that her biopsy happened at the same moment of my fall. Psychic connectedness to the people we love transcends the boundaries of space and time, since they don't follow the same laws for us here. It can be useful to be aware of these kinds of experiences and of our increasing abilities. But some of the pain, moodiness or misery that we are "picking up" is not our own, and we can learn how to protect ourself through strengthening our boundaries.

When we begin these kinds of experiences, we may want more and more. After a while, I realized that what I really wanted when I had them was definition, usefulness and protection. I now often picture or see another person's egg-shaped pattern of energy, or aura as they approach me. As we talk, I am aware that their "egg" is overlapping and sometimes encompassing my "egg." If I don't like what I feel,

I will step back a few feet. Sometimes I'll even put up my hands at about heart level, holding them tactfully away as if playing with the tips of my fingers. When we walk away in separate directions, in my mind's eye I picture them taking all of their "stuff" from their egg back with them. I might even do a "psychic housecleaning" by visualizing my own egg filled with white light.

Telepathic Knowing

Telepathy is so much a part of my everyday life that I never think of myself as being telepathic. I perceive the world as having that telepathic level where we are all connected. Often, just minutes or seconds before my daughter calls me long distance, I will think of her. When I call any of my children, they will often tell me they were "just thinking of me." We love each other and are energetically connected, even though we live hundreds of miles apart.

Sometimes I will be thinking of a song which is playing in my mind, and I will turn on the radio and the song is playing. Or I will stall around when I am leaving the house, and then a package arrives that the delivery person could not have left without my signature. It feels good to be aware of these little telepathic "knowings." It gives me a sense that the world is "put together" more than the evening news would lead us to believe.

We are conditioned early in life to communicate with words. Then our thoughts appear in sequential patterns in our minds and in our speech. A primary sense, telepathy, happens before words and sequential thoughts.

In psychotherapy and counseling this ability to feel what the client is feeling can be of help. In my work as a massage therapist, I can be picking up a feeling that a client is still unaware of and ask them if they might be feeling it right now. My information of a feeling is coming from my own inner life, but I can recognize it as not being my own. If I am trying to figure out in words what their feeling is, then that is not telepathy.

A few times I have been naive enough to "use" my psychic abilities with my family and it has backfired. I found out quickly that I was invading their boundaries, their privacy. I then realized that my false self can't always be out of the way when I am so personally involved. Occasionally now, someone close to me will ask for my help, but I am careful to stay objective — keeping out my own agenda — or I just say I can't do it. Then I offer them the opportunity to hear my opinion. The water gets murky when working on a psychic level with family members. I don't recommend it, and I try to be respectful of others' boundaries and not jump in. This is a hard lesson and requires "psychic maturity" — trusting and knowing intuitively when to speak and when to be silent.

Public Speaking

Higher sense perceptions are spectacular for me when speaking to a group. If I focus on the audience's aura, I see them going from individual auras to one huge egg-shaped aura, encompassing everyone. As the mood changes during a story that I am telling, the group aura changes. When I am finished and everyone claps, the aura breaks back down to individual auras, and as that happens, people get up to leave. The clapping of applause may serve more purposes than we think. I also have a felt sense of my audience, and that intuitively guides me in the direction of my topics and my intensity. And naturally it helps during the question and answer period.

I believe higher sense perceptions such as telepathy and other psychic abilities are natural and that we no longer need to separate them as being unusual, paranormal or supernatural. They are part of our everyday experience. We can thus be more aware of our perceptions, just as we need to become more aware of reality being limited by only our beliefs. The less we limit ourselves through beliefs, the bigger our reality gets. I have asked several other public speakers, and they say that their intuition or higher sense perceptions also guide them in some of the ways I have just described. At this level we experience the feeling of being unified within our self and our audience.

Psychic and Spiritual Healing

When observing an aura before I assist someone in their healing process, small waves or kinks in the aura indicate a problem. Problems can also be seen by comparing the density that I see through the aura. This ability first appeared when I saw a murky or foggy look around another's physical body. If the fog was translucent and evenly consistent overall, the person usually reported feeling balanced and healthy. If I saw a murky disturbance and eventually kinks, it usually indicated that they were having some kind of pain or distress. These disturbances can be smoothed out with a wave of the hand through the area or by placing my hands in the area and "holding" it for 10 or 15 minutes. A good introductory book that explains how to do this is *Your Healing Hands*.

My intuition tells me and I then ask if this person feels they might benefit from (or is armored against) a series of "healing treatments," usually three to five over as many days. If they have children or a safe family member or other close person at home, the best arrangement would be for me to show them how to do what I had done, and then turn it over to the safe person. Or I make arrangements to do it myself and/or organize a volunteer group to take turns visiting and providing this healing assistance to the person who needs it. This can also work well with cancer patients who are receiving chemotherapy.

When working with dying patients, my most rewarding memories are of times we invited the grandchildren from age two and older to do a group healing on the grandparent.

Kids naturally know what is going on and welcome the opportunity.[38a]

You don't have to be clairvoyant to be able to help someone, and being able to see the fields or auras is not necessary. What is necessary is a sincere desire to help the other person. Spiritual healing or "helping" can be transmitted from the "healer" to the "healee" by intent. Many times I have watched hospice nurses putting their arm around a patient's shoulder and the two having eye contact and smiling. The patient's aura brightens immediately, and they usually feel better for hours.

In old paradigm medicine it was believed that the death of a patient meant failure. That created a negative attitude around a dying patient and isolated them. The new paradigm recognizes the fact that our patients sometimes die and that compassion plus safe physical touch is what may help them the most. I have seen dying patients totally contracted in pain, even though they are being given large amounts of narcotics. When I or a nurse gently put our hands on them, they tend to relax, their physical positioning opens up, their coloring gets better and they will announce a little while later that they are free of pain. This is by no means a medical failure. Everyone is going to die someday. If we can help with the quality of their life until then with compassion and touch, I call that a success.

Bioenergy Balancing

"Bioenergy Balancing" was the most generic term I could think of when I opened my practice. I don't consider myself a student of any one particular technique or another. I also do not identify any group or culture as having a monopoly on the energy used in healing. I do know that there is living energy coming through and balancing the energy of the client. Therefore, I call what I do "Bioenergy Balancing."

In a session I visualize a light source coming from the Universe or Higher Power, which is carrying healing energy.

I do not do the balancing — it is being done *through* me. I do not have a planned outcome. And I am not attached to any particular outcome. I believe that it is necessary in any such kind of "psychic" act to step aside and let "Thy will be done."

I center, clearing my outer mind of mental activity. I have a clear intent to help. Then I pray, inviting the healing energy into myself, picturing myself as a hollow tube, with hands on the client where the current will flow. I then usually become aware of warmth or an actual sense of a current flowing out through the palms of my hands. I trust the wisdom of the Higher Process and continue where my hands and my heart take me. Once I am aware of the current — which can take anywhere from two to fifteen minutes — I feel as if I am a child at play. I am not using my intellect to plan what to do next. I am moved by the energy or am just constructively "playing" with it.

During the entire session I rely on a state of Consciousness beyond this one more than I do on any one technique. I was assisting people in this way before I became a massage therapist. The deep massage that I do now is for releasing stress and realigning muscle structure. This type of deep work is more effective with deep slow breath work. The client is coached to actually blow the stress out with the release of the muscle.

Boundaries

When I am in session with a client, I often feel awareness of heat, pain or pressure in the same area they are feeling pain, although not at the same intensity. I have developed a sensitivity to what other people are feeling. Sensitivity is close empathy — an understanding of what the other person is feeling without personally identifying. It is observation and a kind of understanding without taking on their pain. This is a complex area. I am feeling what my client feels, but I do not identify with it as my own. To make sure that I don't identify, I have a ritual at the end of each session of shaking my hands and washing them in cold water to break the connection and reactivate my own healthy boundaries. The term "boundaries" here means distinguishing and keeping out what is not me or mine and holding in place what is.

Before I had my near-death experience, I was a sponge for others' emotional pain. Because I was a wounded adult child, I had never developed healthy boundaries. In my life review during my near-death experience (NDE), I saw myself as a child enmeshed in my mother's pain — both her physical pain and her mental/emotional problems. As an adult, still enmeshed, I could feel other people's pain and thought it was my own. I walled myself off from my mother by putting long-distance physical boundaries between us. For months at a time I would find excuses not to be with her, or I would move to the other side of town and eventually out of state. However, distance alone could not heal my woundedness. I needed to develop healthy boundaries, and at the same time realize that we are all connected.

Learning about psychic abilities, including prayer, rituals such as shaking and washing my hands, using white light in my aura, has given me ways to create healthy boundaries. An even more important way that I have used to help myself is to go back developmentally to where I stopped and give myself a second chance to develop my boundaries in therapy, workshops and in reading the literature on healthy boundaries.

After our spiritual awakenings, for those of us who desire to help others, we need to help and heal ourselves first. We are wounded healers. We may help others, but we may also continue being victims to our own wounds. Functioning in any capacity with any of these higher sense perceptions, we will pick up and possibly not be able to throw off others' problems. We need to define and heal our own boundary distortions before we can function as healthy helping professionals.

I now know when the time is appropriate to focus on my higher sense perceptions. I can open in deep trust to the process because I trust my own judgment. While these psychic signals are in my awareness most of the time, I have the choice to act on and use them or ignore them. I also have the confidence in my own sorting abilities to recognize what is mine and what isn't. If I decide that it is appropriate to act, I then answer in honesty, all the while being in a boundless state of consciousness. I set aside my sense of separateness, my boundaries and join for a time with the other.

This kind of psychic rapport cannot flourish when people conceive of themselves as isolated in thought and feeling. The kind of boundlessness I am referring to leads to a freedom and openness that is rare in most forms of human communication. However, children of abuse do not form healthy boundaries. No matter how developed our psychic ability is, without healthy boundaries to define "me" from "not me," we can get hurt.

If we have unhealthy boundaries, we can be like sponges that absorb the painful conflicted material that others radiate from their inner life. It is clearly not ours, yet we soak it up. And unless we have healthy boundaries, others may absorb whatever of ours that we send back to them. To have a healthy relationship with ourselves and others, we each need healthy boundaries.

——— • ———

References

1. Amodeo J, Wentworth K: **Being Intimate: A Guide To Success-ful Relationships.** Arkana/Penguin, NY, 1986

2. Amodeo J: **Love and Betrayal.** Ballantine, NY, 1994

3. Amodeo J: Chapter 7. Setting our boundaries in **Let's Stop Hurting Each Other: The art of loving well** (working title). Ballantine, NY, 1995

4. Avery N: Sadomasochism: a defense against object loss. *Psychoanalytic Review 64:* 101-109, 1977

5. Barnhill LR: Healthy family systems. *The Family Coordinator.* January, pp. 94-100, 1979

6. Bateson G: **Steps to an Ecology of Mind.** Ballantine, NY, 1972

7. Bateson G: **Mind and Nature.** Dutton, NY, 1979

8. Berenson D: A systemic view of spirituality: God and Twelve-Step programs as resources in family therapy. *Journal for Strategic and Systemic Therapies.* Vol. 9, No. 1, Spring 1990

9. Berenson D: Between I and thou. *Family Therapy Networker,* Sept/Oct, 1990

10. Berkowitz DA: An overview of the psychodynamics of couples: bridging concepts. in Nadelson C & Polonsky D (eds): **Marriage and Divorce: A contemporary perspective,** Guilford Press, NY, 1983

11. Black C: **Double Duty.** Ballantine, NY, 1990

12. Blatt S, Ritzler B: Thought disorder and boundary disturbance in psychosis. *Journal of Consulting and Clinical Psychology 42:* 370-381, 1974

13. Bowen M: **Family Therapy in Clinical Practice.** Jason Aronson, NY, 1978

14. Breeskin AD: **Romaine Brooks.** Smithsonian Institution Press, Washington, D.C., 1986. (also from Morand, P. et al: [The Art of] **Romaine Brooks,** Publ. (in French) unknown, 1967

15. Brodey WM: On the dynamics of narcissism: externalization and early ego development. *Psychoanalytic Study of the Child 20,* 1965

16. Bruyere R, Farrens J: **Healthy Boundaries.** Bon Publishers, Arcadia, CA, 1992

17. Buber M: **I and Thou** (second edition). Charles Scribners Sons, NY, 1958

18. Buber M: **The Knowledge of Man.** Harper & Row, NY, 1965

19. Byron T. Weiner, S: **The Dhammapada: The sayings of the Buddha.** Vintage/Random House, NY, 1976

20. Cashdan S: **Object Relations Therapy: Using the relationship.** WW Norton, NY, 1988

21. Coleman E: Child physical and sexual abuse among chemically dependent individuals. *Journal of Chemical Dependency Treatment 1(1):* 27-38, 1987

22. Coleman E, Schaefer S: Boundaries of sex and intimacy between client and counselor. *Journal of Counseling and Development 64:* 341-344, 1986

23. Colgan P: Assessment of boundary inadequacy in chemically dependent individuals and families. *Journal of Chemical Dependency Treatment 9(1):* 75-90, 1987

24. Colgan P: Treatment of dependency disorders in men: toward a balance of identity and intimacy. *Journal of Chemical Dependency Treatment 1(1):* 205-227, 1987

25. **A Course in Miracles.** Foundation for Inner Peace. Tiburon, CA, 1976

26. Davis M, Wallbridge D: **Boundary and Space: Introduction to the work of D.W. Winnicott.** Brunner/Mazel, NY, 1981

27. Deikman A: **The Observing Self.** Beacon Press, Boston, MA, 1982

28. Derlega VJ, Chaikin AL: **Sharing Intimacy: What we reveal to others & why.** Spectrum/Prentice Hall, NY, 1975

29. Dicks H: Object relations theory and marital studies. *British Journal of Medical Psychology 35:* 125-129, 1963

29a. Eigen M: Chapter 4. Boundaries, in **The Psychotic Core.** Basic Books, NY, 1992

30. Erikson, E.: **Childhood and Society** (2nd ed). Norton, NY, 1963

31. Fischman, L.G.: Dreams, hallucinogenic drug states and schizophrenia: a psychological and biological comparison. *Schizophrenia Bulletin 9(1):* 73-94, 1983

32. Fogarty TF: (several papers, including the following) On emptiness and closeness, Part 1; The distancer and the pursuer; Fusion; Triangles; Evolution of a systems thinker. **Compendium I,** Center for Family Learning, New Rochelle, NY, 1973-78 (Part II is 1978-83)

33. Fossum M, Mason M: **Facing Shame: Families in recovery.** WW Norton, NY, 1986

34. Fraiberg S et. al.: Ghosts in the nursery. *Journal of the American Academy of Child Psychiatry 14:* 387-421, 1975

35. Framo J: Symptoms from a family transactional viewpoint. *International Psychiatry Clinics 7:* 125-171, 1970

36. Frost R: **Selected Poems of Robert Frost** (with introduction by Robert Graves). Holt Rinehart & Winston, NY, 1963

37. Gendlin ET: **Focusing.** Everest House, NY, 1978

38. Giovacchini PL: The persistent psychosis — schizophrenia. *Psychoanalytic Inquiry 3:1:9-36,* 1983

38a. Gordon R: **Your Healing Hands: The polarity experience.** Unity Press, Santa Cruz, CA, 1978

39. Gray WG: **Inner Traditions of Magic.** Samuel Weiser, York Beach, ME, 1970

40. Gruen A: **The Betrayal of the Self: The fear of autonomy in men & women.** Grove Press, NY, 1986

41. Guntrip H: **Psychoanalytic Theory, Therapy and the Self: A basic guide to the human personality in Freud, Erikson, Klein, Sullivan, Fairbairn, Hartmann, Jacobson & Winnicott.** Basic Books/Harper Torchbooks, NY, 1971

42. Harris B, Bascom L: **Full Circle: The near death experience and beyond.** Pocket Books, Simon & Schuster, 1990

43. Harris B: **Spiritual Awakenings: A guidebook for experiencers.** Stage 3 Books, 31 Walker Ave., Ste. 100, Baltimore, MD 21208, 1993

44. Harris B: **Personal Communication,** Baltimore, 1992

45. Hazelden booklet: Setting Boundaries: A moment to reflect. Hazelden, Center City, MN, 1989

46. Hoffman E: **Visions of Innocence.** Shambhala, Boston, 1992

47. Horney K: **Neurosis and Human Growth.** Norton, NY, 1950

48. Horney K: **The Neurotic Personality of Our Time.** Norton, NY, 1952

48a. Huxley A: **The Perennial Philosophy.** Harper & Row, NY, 1945 & 1971

49. James M: Diagnosis and treatment of ego state boundary problems. *Tranactional Analysis Journal 16(3):* 188-196, 1986

50. Jordan JV: Empathy and Self-Boundaries. (Work in Progress No. 16). Stone Center for Developmental Services and Studies, Wellesley College, MA, 1984

51. Karpman SB: Fairy tales and script drama analysis. *Transactional Analysis Bulletin,* 7:26:39-40, April, 1968

51a. Kaschak E: Chapter 6. Limits & Boundaries, in **Engendered Lives: A new psychology of womens' experience.** Basic Books, NY, 1992

52. Katherine A: **Boundaries: Where you end and I begin.** Parkside Publishing, Park Ridge, IL, 1991

53. Kellogg T, with Harrison, M.: **Broken Toys Broken Dreams: Understanding co-dependency, compulsive behavior and family.** BRAT, Amherst, MA, 1990

54. Kerr ME, Bowen M: **Family Evaluation: An approach based on Bowen Theory.** WW Norton, NY, 1988

55. Klein M: Notes on some schizoid mechanisms. *Developments,* 1952

56. Kohut H: **The Analysis of the Self.** International University Press, NY, 1971

57. Landis B: Ego Boundaries. *Psychological Issues 6(4) monograph 24:* 1-177, International University Press, NY, 1970

57a. Lao-tzu: **The Tao te Ching.** Numerous translations are available, such as: Gura-Fue Feng & Jan English's Vintage/Random House, NY, 1972; and Lin Yutang's, Modern Literary/Random House, 1948

57b. Lazaris: Releasing negative ego (taped talk). Concept Synergy, Palm Beach, 1986 (407-588-9599)

58. Lerner H et al: Patterns of ego boundary disturbance in neurotic, borderline and schizophrenic patients. *Psychoanalytic Psychology 2(1):* 47-66, 1985

59. Lerner R: Boundaries for co-dependents. (Booklet 5217). Hazelden, Center City, MN, 1988

60. Levin P: **Cycles of Power: A user's guide to the seven seasons of life.** Health Communications, Deerfield Beach, FL, 1988

61. Levinson DJ et al: **The Season's of a Man's Life.** Ballantine, NY, 1978

62. Lewis L, Schilling KM: Gestalt concepts of ego boundary and responsibility: a critical review. *Psychotherapy 15(3):* 272-276, 1978

63. Lidz T et al: **Schizophrenia and the Family.** International University Press, NY, 1965

64. Lowen A: **Narcissism: Denial of the true self.** Collier/Macmillan, NY, 1985

65. Maeder T: Wounded healers. *The Atlantic,* Jan, pp. 37-47, 1989

66. Mahler M et al: **The Psychological Birth of the Human Infant.** Basic Books, NY, 1975

67. Main TF: Mutual projection in a marriage. *Comprehensive Psychiatry 7:* 432-449, 1966

68. Malin A, Grotstein JS: Projective identification in the therapeutic process. *International Journal of Psychoanalysis,* 47(1) 26-31, 1966

69. Malone TP, Malone PT: **The Art of Intimacy.** Prentice Hall, NY, 1987

70. Maslow A: **Toward a Psychology of Being.** Van Nostrand, Princeton, NJ, 1961

71. Mason M: Intimacy. (booklet) Hazelden, Center City, MN, 1986

72. Masson JM: **The Assault on Truth: Freud's suppression of the seduction theory.** Farrar, Straus, and Giroux, NY, 1984

73. Masterson JF: **The Search for the Real Self: Unmasking the personality disorders of our age.** Free Press/MacMillan, NY, 1988

74. McCann IL, Pearlman LA: **Psychological Trauma and the Adult Survivor: Theory, therapy, transformation.** Brunner/Mazel, NY, 1991

75. McCann E, Shannon D: **The Two Step: The dance toward intimacy.** Grove Press, NY, 1985

76. McGill ME: **Male Intimacy.** Perennial/Harper & Row, San Francisco, 1985

77. McKeon J, Wong B: The Manual for Life. (booklet) PD Seminars, Gabriola Island, BC, Canada, 1990

78. Miller A: **The Drama of the Gifted Child.** Basic Books/Harper Colophon, NY, 1981

79. Minuchin S: **Families and Family Therapy.** Harvard University Press, Cambridge, MA, 1974. Also **Family Therapy Techniques,** Harvard University Press

80. Minuchin S et. al.: **Families of the Slums.** Basic, NY, 1967

81. Mitchell J: **The Selected Melanie Klein.** Free Press, NY, 1987

82. Montagu A: **Touching: The human significance of skin.** Harper & Row, NY, 1971

83. Napier AY, Whitaker CA: **The Family Crucible: The intense experience of family therapy.** Harper & Row, NY, 1978

84. Nouwen H: **The Wounded Healer.** Doubleday, NY, 1973

85. Ogden TH: **Projective Identification and Psychotherapeutic Technique.** Jason Aronson, NY, 1991

86. Paine-Gernee K, Hunt T: **Emotional Healing: A program for emotional sobriety.** Warner, NY, 1990

87. Palombo J: Critique of Schamess' concept of boundaries. *Clinical Social Work Journal 15(3):* 284-293, 1987

88. Peterson MR: **At Personal Risk: Boundary violations in pro-fessional-client relationships.** WW Norton, NY, 1992

89. Pick TM: A fusion/separation model of psychotherapy. *Psychotherapy 23:* 390-394, 1986

90. Polster S: Ego boundary as process: a systemic contextual ap-proach. *Psychiatry 46:* 247-257, 1983

91. Quinlan D, Harrow M: Boundary disturbance in schizophrenia, *Journal of Abnormal Psychology 83:* 533-541, 1974

92. Ring K: **Heading Toward Omega: In search of the meaning of the near-death experience.** Wm Morrow, NY, 1984

93. Rodegast P, Stanton J: **Emmanuel's Book II: The choice for Love.** Bantam, NY, 1989

94. Roland A: Psychoanalysis without interpretation: psychoanalytic therapy in Japan. *Contemporary Psychoanalysis 19(3):* 499-505, 1983

95. Sandler J et al: **The Patient and the Analyst: The basis of the psychoanalytic process.** International University Press, NY, 1973

96. Satir V: **Conjoint Family Therapy.** Science and Behavior Books, Palo Alto, CA, 1987

97. Segal H: **Introduction to the Work of Melanie Klein.** Basic Books, NY, 1964

98. Scarf M: **Intimate Partners: Patterns in Love & Marriage.** Random House, NY, 1987

99. Scharff DE, Scharff JS: Therapeutic Uses of the Self (Workshop). Sheppard Pratt Hospital, 14 Jan, 1992

100. Schamess G: Boundary issues in countertransference: a developmental perspective. *Clinical Social Work Journal 9:* 244-257, 1981

100a. Smith M: **When I Say No I Feel Guilty.** Bantam, NY, 1975

101. Stoltz SG: Beware of boundary issues. *Transactional Analysis Journal 15(1):* 37-41, 1985

102. Utain M: Stepping Out of Chaos: Recovery for incest survivors, adult children and co-dependents, (booklet), Health Communications, Deerfield Beach, FL, 1989. Material also in her book *Scream Louder,* 1989

103. Wallace E: Conventional boundaries or protective temenos. *Art Psychotherapy 1:* 91-99, 1973

104. Weddige RL: The hidden psychotherapeutic dilemma: spouse of the borderline. *American Journal of Psychotherapy XL(1):* 52-61, 1986

105. Weinberg G, Rowe D: **The Projection Principle.** St. Martin's Press, NY, 1988

106. Wegsheider S: **Another Chance: Hope and health for the alcoholic family.** Science and Behavior Books, Palo Alto, CA, 1981

107. Weinhold BK, Weinhold JB: **Breaking Free of the Co-dependency Trap.** Stillpoint, Walpole, NH, 1989

108. Whitaker TC: (This quote attributed to Terry Cole Whitaker, San Diego, date unknown.)

109. Whitfield CL: **Healing The Child Within: Discovery and recovery for adult children of dysfunctional families.** Health Communications, Deerfield Beach, FL, 1987

110. Whitfield CL: **Spirituality in Recovery** (formerly Alcoholism and Spirituality). Perrin & Treggett 1338 Rt 206, Stillman, NJ, 08558, 1985 (800-321-7911)

111. Whitfield CL: The Spiritual Psychology of Jesus Christ: An introduction to what he really taught and continues to teach. (booklet) Perrin & Treggett, address above, 1992

112. Whitfield CL: **Co-dependence: Healing the human condition,** Health Communications, Deerfield Beach, FL, 1991

113. Whitfield CL: Co-alcoholism, addictions and related disorders. In Lowinson JH, Ruiz P, Millman RB (eds): **Comprehensive Textbook of Substance Abuse.** Williams & Wilkins, Baltimore, 1992

114. Whitfield CL: **Feelings.** (working title of book in progress for 1995)

115. Whitfield CL: **Wisdom to Know the Difference: Transforming Co-dependence into healthy relationships** (working title of book in progress) for 1995 or later

116. Whitfield CL: **A Gift To Myself: A personal workbook and guide to healing my Child Within.** Health Communications, Deerfield Beach, FL, 1990

117. Whitfield CL: My Recovery Plan — For Stage 1, 2 and 3 Recovery, (booklets). Health Communications, Deerfield Beach, FL, 1992-93

118. Whitfield CL: Boundaries in Counseling & Therapy, (working title of booklet). Health Communications, Deerfield Beach, FL, 1994

119. Wilber K: **No Boundary.** Shambhala, Boulder, CO, 1978

120. Wills-Brandon C: **Learning To Say No: Establishing Healthy Boundaries.** Health Communications, Deerfield Beach, FL, 1990

121. Wills-Brandon C: Where Do I Draw the Line? How to get past other people's problems and start living your own life (a mini-workbook on boundaries). Health Communications, Deerfield Beach, FL, 1991

122. Wood BL: **Children of Alcoholism: The struggle for self and intimacy in adult life.** University Press, NY, 1987

123. Wynne L: Indications and contradictions for exploratory family therapy. In Boszormenyi-Nagy & F Framo (eds): **Intensive Family Therapy, Theoretical and Practical Aspects.** Hoeber, NY, 1963

124. Zerof HG: **Finding Intimacy: The art of happiness in living together.** Winston/Harper & Row, San Francisco, 1978

125. Zinner J: The implications of projective identification for marital interaction. in H Grunebaum and J Christ (eds): **Marriage Problems and Prospects.** Little Brown, Boston, 1977

126. Zinner J, Shapiro R: Projective identification as a mode of perception and behavior in families of aolescents. *International Journal of Psychoanalysis 53:* 523-530, 1972

Index

Other Books By . . .
Health Communications

ADULT CHILDREN OF ALCOHOLICS (Expanded)
Janet Woititz
Over a year on *The New York Times* Best-Seller list, this book is the primer on Adult Children of Alcoholics.
ISBN 1-55874-112-7   **$8.95**

STRUGGLE FOR INTIMACY
Janet Woititz
Another best-seller, this book gives insightful advice on learning to love more fully.
ISBN 0-932194-25-7   **$6.95**

BRADSHAW ON: THE FAMILY: A Revolutionary Way of Self-Discovery
John Bradshaw
The host of the nationally televised series of the same name shows us how families can be healed and individuals can realize full potential.
ISBN 0-932194-54-0   **$9.95**

HEALING THE SHAME THAT BINDS YOU
John Bradshaw
This important book shows how toxic shame is the core problem in our compulsions and offers new techniques of recovery vital to all of us.
ISBN 0-932194-86-9   **$9.95**

HEALING THE CHILD WITHIN: Discovery and Recovery for
Adult Children of Dysfunctional Families — Charles Whitfield, M.D.
Dr. Whitfield defines, describes and discovers how we can reach our Child Within to heal and nurture our woundedness.
ISBN 0-932194-40-0   **$8.95**

A GIFT TO MYSELF: A Personal Guide To Healing My Child Within
Charles L. Whitfield, M.D.
Dr. Whitfield provides practical guidelines and methods to work through the pain and confusion of being an Adult Child of a dysfunctional family.
ISBN 1-55874-042-2   **$11.95**

HEALING TOGETHER: A Guide To Intimacy And Recovery For
Co-dependent Couples — Wayne Kritsberg, M.A.
This is a practical book that tells the reader why he or she gets into dysfunctional and painful relationships, and then gives a concrete course of action on how to move the relationship toward health.
ISBN 1-55784-053-8   **$8.95**

3201 S.W. 15th Street,
Deerfield Beach, FL 33442-8190
1-800-851-9100

Health
Communications, Inc.